Chicago Tribune

HAWKS DYNASTY

THE CHICAGO BLACKHAWKS' RUN TO THE 2015 STANLEY CUP

Chicago Tribune

Tony W. Hunter, CEO & Publisher

Gerould W. Kern,
Senior Vice President, Editor

Peter Kendall, Managing Editor

Colin McMahon, Associate Editor

George Papajohn, Investigations Editor

Geoff Brown, Operations &
Development Editor

Margaret Holt, Standards Editor

R. Bruce Dold, Editorial Page Editor

John P. McCormick, Deputy
Editorial Page Editor

Marcia Lythcott, Commentary Editor

Amy Carr, Development Editor

Associate Managing Editors for News

   Robin Daughtridge, Photography

   Mark Jacob, Metro

   Mike Kellams, Business

   Cristi Kempf, Editing & Presentation

   Joe Knowles, Sports

HAWKS DYNASTY

This book is book is available in quantity
at special discounts for your group or
organization.

For further information, contact:

Triumph Books
814 North Franklin Street
Chicago, Illinois 60610
Phone: (312) 337-0747
www.triumphbooks.com

Printed in U.S.A.
ISBN: 978-1-62937-064-4

Content packaged by Mojo Media, Inc.
Joe Funk: Editor
Jason Hinman: Creative Director

Front and back cover photos by Brian
Cassella/Chicago Tribune.

Patrick Kane points to his teammates as he celebrates his
third-period goal in Game 6 of the Stanley Cup final at the
United Center. (Brian Cassella/Chicago Tribune)

CONTENTS

For the first time since 1938, the Blackhawks celebrate a Stanley Cup championship on their home ice after winning Game 6 of the Cup final over Tampa Bay on June 15, 2015. (John J. Kim/Chicago Tribune)

INTRODUCTION

For those of us who lived through the previous "golden era" of Blackhawks hockey, the team's recent ascendance is at once familiar and strange.

In the days of Bobby Hull and Stan Mikita, the Hawks were a hot ticket – just like now – and the old Stadium was always full – just like now. But back then, with only six teams in the entire National Hockey League (and only four of those six in the U.S.), being a fan felt more like belonging to a cult.

Despite the fact that they competed against a much smaller field (only six teams comprised the NHL until the 1967-68 season, when the league doubled in size to 12 teams), those great Hawks teams of the 1960s and '70s managed to win just one Stanley Cup, in 1961. Compare that to the current Blackhawks, who had to fend off 29 other teams for the right to hoist the Cup – a feat they accomplished three times in six seasons, creating a generation of new fans who form what we now know as Blackhawk Nation.

These Blackhawks also have to deal with the glare and heat of an always-on media machine; the home games of the Hull-Mikita era were not even televised locally. Consider the contrast to today, when every play – good and bad – is replayed and dissected in real time across multiple media platforms.

There are many reasons to celebrate these Blackhawks, to savor this run of championships that surely qualifies them as a modern-era dynasty. But the best reason is this: Who knows when we will see the likes of this team again?

With that in mind, we put together the book you hold in your hands. It is meant to mark a special moment in time, this unprecedented era – a new ice age, if you will – when the Blackhawks stood front and center in the hearts and minds of Chicago sports fans. Hawks Dynasty contains a wealth of magnificent images from the Tribune's team of award-winning photographers as well as stories by the sports staff, all of which chronicle the team's amazing quest to reclaim a title that had so cruelly eluded them a year before. Designed and produced by our friends at Triumph Books, Hawks Dynasty expertly captures the drama and excitement of a truly unforgettable season.

Don't let the glow of this golden era fade. Relive it through these pages, and remember it fondly forever, because history tells us that someday – probably sooner than we'd like – these, too, will be the good old days.

Joe Knowles
Associate Managing Editor / Sports
Chicago Tribune

Marian Hossa (center) is mobbed by teammates after the Blackhawks' 2-0 victory over Tampa Bay in Game 6 of the 2015 Stanley Cup final. (Brian Cassella/Chicago Tribune)

For the third time in six seasons, the Blackhawks pose with the Stanley Cup for the traditional on-ice team photo. (Brian Cassella/Chicago Tribune)

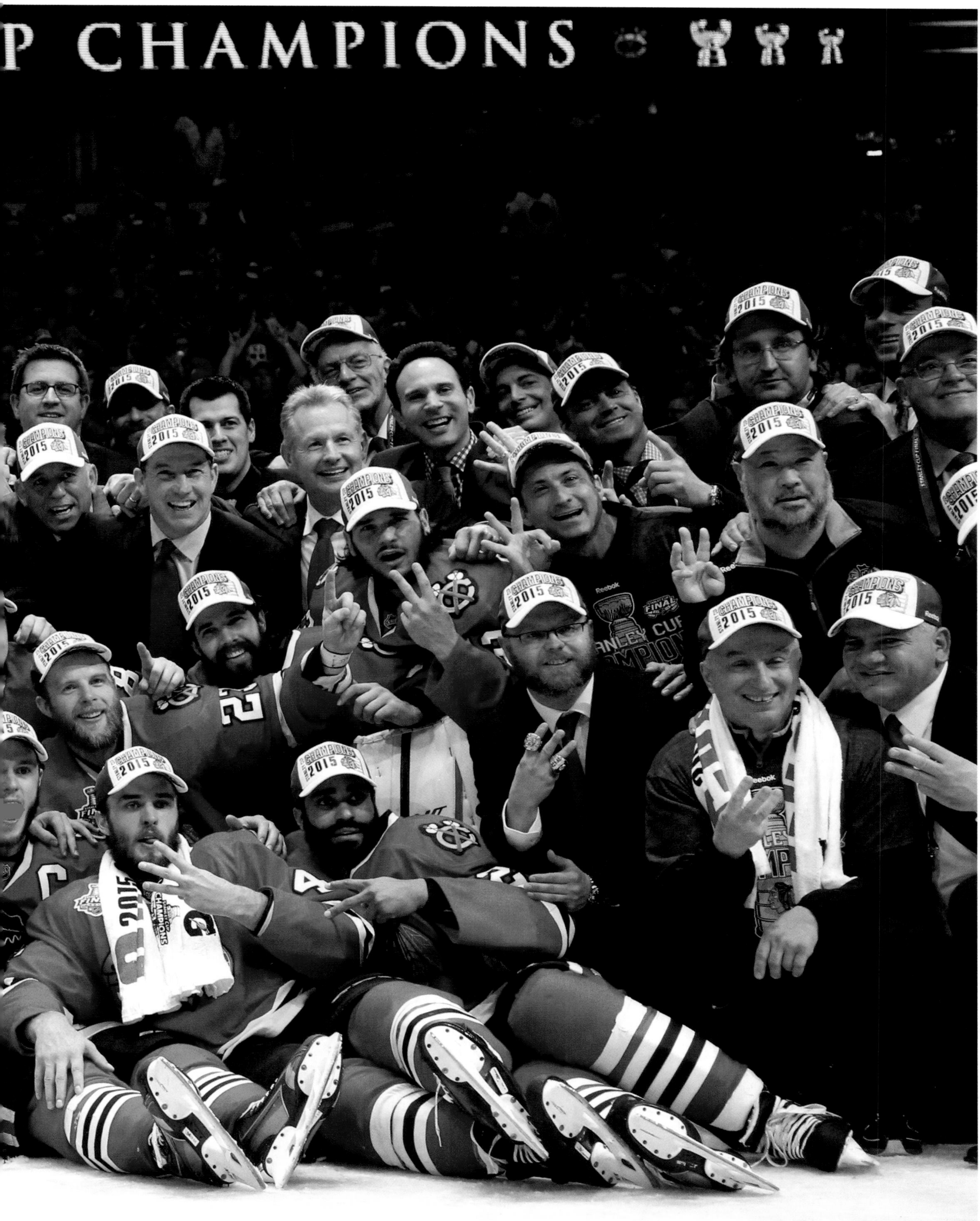
P CHAMPIONS

Game 1
June 3, 2015
Blackhawks 2, Lightning 1

FANTASTIC FINNISH

Teravainen, Vermette strike 1:58 apart in 3rd as Hawks prevail

By Chris Kuc

Even before Tesla coils sent jolts of electricity high above the ice, Amalie Arena was super-charged in anticipation of Game 1 of the 2015 Stanley Cup Final.

The Blackhawks saved their burst of energy for the end and rallied to stun the Lightning 2-1 and take home-ice advantage in the series.

Teuvo Teravainen and Antoine Vermette scored 1 minute, 58 seconds apart late in the third period to make a winner of goaltender Corey Crawford. Alex Killorn had a highlight-reel goal early in the first period for the Lightning, but Ben Bishop couldn't make it hold up.

"Tampa was all over us in the first," Teravainen said. "Myself, I got better and our team got better all the time in the game. Huge two goals and a great win."

The first surprise of the series occurred during pregame warmups when Bryan Bickell wasn't on the ice and fellow winger Kris Versteeg was. After not playing the final two periods of Game 7 of the Western Conference finals against the Ducks, Bickell practiced Tuesday and participated in Wednesday's morning skate. Heading into Game 1 of the finals, it was uncertain as to whether Bickell had suffered an injury or if coach Joel Quenneville held him out against the Ducks because of poor play.

"We'll say it was my decision but we'll say a little bit of both," Quenneville said Monday when asked if Bickell was benched or injured.

After Wednesday's game he said Bickell had an upper-body injury.

The Lightning displayed their skill early on Killorn's goal at 4:31 of the first. The forward baffled Crawford by batting in a floating puck with a brilliant backhander to send another jolt of energy into the crowd.

The game reached deep into the third before the Hawks struck at 13:28 to stun the crowd of 19,204. First, Teravainen sent a shot from the left circle that sailed past a screened Bishop. Vermette

Patrick Sharp raises his arms in celebration as he watches a shot by Antoine Vermette land in the Lightning net behind goalie Ben Bishop. Vermette's third-period goal broke a 1-1 tie and proved to be the game-winner as the Blackhawks took a 1-0 lead in the series. (Brian Cassella/Chicago Tribune)

then gave the Hawks a 2-1 advantage when he wristed a shot from the slot.

Playing in his first Cup final game, Teravainen said he sought advice of some Hawks teammates about what to expect but otherwise is taking the experience as it comes.

"I just have to think it's like normal and do all the same things," the rookie forward said. "I'm just trying to enjoy everything."

He certainly enjoyed his third-period goal that helped the Hawks to the huge victory in Game 1. ●

Above: Kris Versteeg sprawls to the ice after crashing into the post on a rush to the net in the second period of Game 1 in Tampa. (Brian Cassella/Chicago Tribune) Opposite: Antoine Vermette (left) scores the go-ahead goal in the third period of Game 1 in Tampa. The Hawks took control with a pair of goals in a span of less than two minutes. (Brian Cassella/Chicago Tribune)

STANLEY CUP FINAL

Game 2
June 6, 2015
Lightning 4, Blackhawks 3

SPLIT SECOND

Sharp has company
in blame game

By Chris Kuc

It was a night at the races.

The Blackhawks and Lightning burst out of the gate and sprinted up and down the ice during Game 2 of the Stanley Cup Final at Amalie Arena.

In a fast and furious affair, the Lightning reached the wire first for a scintillating 4-3 victory over the Hawks to even the best-of-seven series at 1-1.

The Lightning avoided heading to Chicago for Games 3 and 4 in a 2-0 series hole. Jason Garrison had a goal – the game-winner in the third period – and an assist, Nikita Kucherov scored and added a helper, and Tyler Johnson and Cedric Paquette also had goals.

Backup goaltender Andrei Vasilevskiy earned the victory in relief of starter Ben Bishop, who twice left the ice during the third period for an unexplained reason.

"We expected a fast pace," Hawks captain Jonathan Toews said. "We know we can play at that pace. We let them get a little too comfortable with their rush game in the second (period) and gave up a few too many of those odd-man rushes and some high quality scoring chances."

Andrew Shaw, Teuvo Teravainen and Brent Seabrook scored for the Hawks, but they weren't able to complete a second consecutive comeback as Corey Crawford suffered the loss.

"Sometimes those ones slip away from you," Toews said. "We just kept giving up goals every time we got ourselves back into it. We just ran out of time."

Garrison scored the winner on the power play after Sharp was whistled for two consecutive penalties early in the third, the latter of which proved costly.

"I don't think I've ever done that before," Sharp said. "It happened. You move on from it. I take responsibility and apologize to our penalty killers for putting them under such stress."

Despite the loss, the Hawks accomplished what they set out to do when they arrived in Tampa: Win at least one to seize home-ice advantage.

"It's definitely a good position," said Crawford, who made 20 saves. "We'll go home for Game 3 and we have a lot of confidence.

"It's going to be tough, but we're going to be ready to battle."

Added Toews: "To go home tied 1-all, I don't think is something we're satisfied with considering the position we were in going into (Game 2), but we're excited to go back to our building." ●

Things were looking up for Brandon Saad and the Blackhawks after Teuvo Teravainen scored in the second period of Game 2 to give the Hawks a 2-1 lead, but Tampa Bay prevailed 5-4 to even the series. (Anthony Souffle/Chicago Tribune)

STANLEY CUP FINAL

Game 3
June 8, 2015
Lightning 3, Blackhawks 2

MISSING TARGET

Bishop looks like easy mark,
but Hawks can't take advantage

By Chris Kuc

With the opposing goaltender clearly hampered by an injury, the Blackhawks did exactly what they should by swarming the offensive zone and throwing everything at the net during the first period of Game 3 of the Stanley Cup Final.

Then the Hawks stopped throwing much of anything at Lightning goalie Ben Bishop, and they left the ice having dropped a 3-2 heartbreaker at the United Center. They now trail the best-of-seven series 2-1.

"We fired lots of shots right at the beginning and after they played a little bit in our zone, and we stopped shooting pucks at him," Hawks winger Marian Hossa said. "If he's not OK, we should take advantage of it and just keep peppering the puck at the net like we did in the first period."

They didn't and it cost them. Bishop left in the third period of Game 2 with an unspecified injury that has cost him movement in the crease. After bombarding him with 19 shots in the first, the Hawks managed only 19 more during the final two periods combined.

"(Bishop) looks like he's got some issues," Hawks coach Joel Quenneville said. "We still didn't put enough pucks at the net and traffic, obviously. Certainly later in the game there we made it easier on him."

Little came easy for the Hawks. Even after Brandon Saad scored early in the third to give them a 2-1 lead, the Lightning struck right back with a goal by Ondrej Palat 13 seconds later.

Cedric Paquette scored the winner with 3 minutes, 11 seconds remaining when he stuffed a loose puck past Corey Crawford, and the home-ice advantage the Hawks had seized with a Game 1 victory was lost.

"(When) you grab momentum after a goal, you want to build on that," Crawford said. "Giving up a goal after that is not what we want."

In addition to the goals by Palat and Paquette, the Lightning got a score from Ryan Callahan to give Bishop just enough offense to prevail. Brad Richards also scored for the Hawks, but Crawford (29 saves) failed to hold the lead.

The loss put the Hawks on their heels, though they can draw on the experience of falling behind the Bruins 2-1 in the finals in 2013 before storming back to win in six games.

"We've been down a few times, even in the last series against Anaheim," Hossa said. "We've been in this situation. I thought we played a pretty solid game, but we have to give (the Lightning) credit. They're a great team and they're battling. We did pretty well tonight, but a few mistakes cost us." ●

Corey Crawford can't keep Ryan Callahan's shot in front of him during the first period of Game 3 at the United Center. Callahan's goal opened the scoring just 5 minutes and 9 seconds into the game. (Brian Cassella/Chicago Tribune)

STANLEY CUP FINAL

Game 4
June 10, 2015
Blackhawks 2, Lightning 1

THRILL-SQUEAKER

Saad breaks tie in 3rd, Crawford weathers storm to even series

By Chris Kuc

Two hit posts and one off the crossbar into Game 4 of the Stanley Cup Final, it appeared the Blackhawks were destined to fall perilously close to the end of their season.

Then a bounce finally went their way – in Brandon Saad's direction, to be exact – and the Hawks eventually were able to celebrate a 2-1 victory over the Lightning at the United Center.

Saad scored 6 minutes, 22 seconds into the third period and goaltender Corey Crawford withstood a furious Lightning flurry in the waning seconds to help the Hawks even the best-of-seven series 2-2 with Game 5 in Tampa.

"It was really pretty lucky," said Saad, who corralled a loose puck in the slot, kicked it to his stick and got just enough of a backhander to send it into the net. "I just saw space going to the net, tried to drive and create some chaos. The goalie made a good play with poking the puck; it bounced around my feet and finally found my stick. I just tried to get some wood on it and get it to the net and it found a way through his legs."

Jonathan Toews also scored and Crawford turned aside 24 shots to lift his often-sluggish teammates to the victory before a nerve-wracked crowd of 22,354. Crawford outdueled an unlikely foe at the other end of the ice as 20-year-old Andrei Vasilevskiy was a surprise starter for the Lightning with No. 1 goalie Ben Bishop sidelined with an undisclosed injury.

Alex Killorn had the goal for the Lightning, but the Hawks clamped down defensively in the third period and withstood an onslaught of shots in the final moments, including one from Steven Stamkos from the slot on which Crawford stoned the Lightning captain.

Saad's goal never would have happened if not for a quick and subtle play by teammate Brad Richards. The veteran center used his stick to tie up Lightning defenseman Anton Stralman and pave the way for Saad to get to the front of the net where he finished the deal and sent the crowd into a frenzy.

"I had to pick the stick so Saader could get to

Brandon Saad celebrates his go-ahead goal in the third period of Game 4. Saad's goal — his second in two games and eighth of the postseason — gave the Blackhawks a 2-1 victory and evened the series at 2 games apiece. (Nuccio DiNuzzo/Chicago Tribune)

the net," Richards said. "I don't think I invented that play but it worked."

It was one of the few things that worked for the Hawks, who were sluggish through much of the game but displayed enough mettle finally to solve Vasilevskiy and even the series.

"That was probably our worst game in a while, for whatever reason," Richards said. "We really wanted it but we just kept getting in each other's way. (The Lightning) are way better than anybody imagined at checking and trying to frustrate you.

"You have those nights. The good thing is we're experienced enough and good enough that we got through it. We got big plays by different people and big saves and then we got going." ●

Above: Jonathan Toews tries to settle down the puck and direct it toward the Tampa Bay net. Toews didn't score on this play, but his second-period goal gave the Blackhawks a 1-0 lead in Game 4. (Nuccio DiNuzzo/ Chicago Tribune) Opposite: Antoine Vermette and Cedric Paquette get tangled up along the boards during the first period of Game 4 at the United Center. (Nuccio DiNuzzo/ Chicago Tribune)

STANLEY CUP FINAL

Game 5
June 13, 2015
Blackhawks 2, Lightning 1

CHICAGO HOPE

Hawks 1 victory from winning Cup in front of home crowd

By Chris Kuc

They didn't get the opportunity in 2010. Or in 2013.

But thanks to their 2-1 victory over the Lightning in Game 5 of the Stanley Cup Final at Amalie Arena, the Blackhawks have a chance to do something they haven't done since 1938: win the Stanley Cup in Chicago.

Antoine Vermette scored the winner early in the third period and Corey Crawford continued to amaze in goal to lift the Hawks to a 3-2 advantage in the series and put the franchise on the brink of its sixth Cup overall and third in the last six seasons.

The Cup will be in the United Center for Game 6 when the Hawks will try to clinch in front of the fan base that has sold out 327 consecutive games, including 57 in the postseason.

Patrick Sharp also had a goal and Crawford bested counterpart Ben Bishop as the Hawks clawed out another one-goal victory. Each game of the series has been decided by a single score. Valtteri Filppula had the Lightning goal, but a continued strong defensive effort and a poised and locked-in Crawford (31 saves) pushed the Hawks to the crucial victory.

History is on the Hawks' side. The team that has won Game 5 after a split of the first four games of the final has gone on to capture the Cup 16 of 23 times since the series went to a best-of-seven format in 1939.

That and the way they have overcome much of what the Lightning have thrown at them has the Hawks cautiously optimistic and pondering circling the ice with the Cup held aloft while fans at the United Center celebrate with them.

"It's easy to daydream sometimes, and all of a sudden, you're thinking of winning the Cup and hoisting (it) and all the things that come with it," captain Jonathan Toews said. "We have to try to get those thoughts out of our heads and just focus on the task."

A pair of goalie miscues in the early going – one at each end of the ice – proved calamitous for the Lightning in Game 5. First, Crawford misfired on a clearing attempt and sent it right to Nikita Kucherov. The winger pounced, but a diving Crawford got his body on the shot, and in the process Kucherov was sent flying into the left post. He appeared to injure his shoulder and did not return for the remainder of the game.

Antoine Vermette (right) and Teuvo Teravainen celebrate Vermette's third-period goal in Game 5 at Amalie Arena in Tampa. Vermette's goal proved to be the difference in a 2-1 Blackhawks victory over the Lightning. (Brian Cassella/Chicago Tribune)

A short time later, Bishop made things worse for the Lightning. The goalie wandered far out of the crease to play the puck and collided with teammate Victor Hedman. The puck popped right to Sharp, who cruised in and tucked it into the open net.

Midway through the second, the Lightning tied it 1-1 when Filppula corralled a terrific cross-ice pass from Jason Garrison and ripped it past Crawford.

Vermette scored the winner when he crashed the net and fired in a rebound of a Kris Versteeg shot two minutes into the third.

Hawks coach Joel Quenneville anticipates happy days ahead for Chicago.

"(We've) never been in this spot," he said. "I'm sure it will be crazy over the next two days in town. The buzz will be off the charts. (I) look forward to it." ●

Above: Lightning goalie Ben Bishop makes the initial save on a shot by Kris Versteeg (23), but the rebound would land on the stick of Antoine Vermette, who banged it home for the go-ahead goal in Game 5. (Nuccio DiNuzzo/Chicago Tribune) Opposite: Corey Crawford makes one of his 31 saves in the Blackhawks' 2-1 victory in Game 5. (Brian Cassella/Chicago Tribune)

STANLEY CUP FINAL

Game 6
June 15, 2015
Blackhawks 2, Lightning 0

PUCK DYNASTY

With third Cup in six years, Blackhawks
leave no room for doubt

By Chris Kuc

They did it under the five Stanley Cup banners hanging from the rafters.

They did it under the banners honoring legends Glenn Hall, Pierre Pilote, Keith Magnuson, Bobby Hull, Denis Savard, Stan Mikita and Tony Esposito.

The Blackhawks did it at home.

For the first time in 77 years, the Hawks celebrated winning a Stanley Cup in Chicago after they topped the Lightning 2-0 in Game 6 in front of 22,424 delirious fans at the United Center.

Patrick Kane had a goal and an assist, Duncan Keith also scored and goaltender Corey Crawford made 25 saves to help lift the Hawks to their third Cup in the last six seasons.

"This one is special because we did it in front of our fans," said Keith, who was awarded the Conn Smythe Trophy as the most valuable player of the postseason. "Third time winning the Cup in six years, that's unreal."

It's a feeling that never gets old, even for those who will be adding a third ring to their collections.

"It's the greatest feeling in the world," coach Joel Quenneville said. "Once you do it once, you can't wait to do it again. It was special doing it in front of our own fans. The building was electric. The town had a buzz to it."

The Hawks reeled off three consecutive victories to capture the best-of-seven series 4-2 and finished the season a perfect 33-0 when leading in games after two periods.

While 2010 and '13 were amazing moments, to win it at home in front of fans who seemed intent on losing their voices from the opening notes to the national anthem until each Hawks player hoisted the Cup over their heads on the United Center, made this one all the more cherished.

"We love this city, we love the crowd, they're spoiling us every year with sellouts," winger Marian Hossa said. "We're just so happy to be able to give this back to the city and the people who love the Blackhawks."

Added captain Jonathan Toews: "We wanted it for each other (and) for the city. Winning a championship like this in your own city in some ways transcends the sport. Everyone wants to be a part of it. It's amazing.

Duncan Keith celebrates his second-period goal, which broke a scoreless tie in Game 6 and proved to be the Cup-clincher. (Anthony Souffle/Chicago Tribune)

You can feel the energy."

The celebration continued throughout Chicagoland as new and long-time fans alike joined the party.

"After we won our second one, we said ultimately if you could ever win one here in Chicago that would be the ultimate Stanley Cup," team president John McDonough said. "I think they're going to be celebrating in Chicago the entire summer."

The Lightning did not go easily in Game 6 as the Hawks had to work for every inch of ice. After a scoreless – and nervous – opening period, Keith sent the crowd into a frenzy when he scored in the waning moments of the second. The two-time Norris Trophy winner fired a long shot that Lightning goalie Ben Bishop stopped but yielded a rebound. Like a point guard following his shot, Keith swooped in and batted the rebound past Bishop's glove.

That set off the first chants of "We Want the Cup! We Want the Cup!" from the Hawks faithful.

They were heard again when Kane made it 2-0. With the Hawks clinging to the lead late in the third, the winger Kane snapped a six-game goalless skid when he took a terrific cross-slot pass from Brad Richards (two assists) and fired in a one-timer from the right circle to set off a raucous celebration that lasted well into the night.

"Our goal was to get one and try to get the franchise on the right track and get this orchestrated and the process and the system and everything together and hire the right people," McDonough said. "Apparently, we have. What a reward for the city of Chicago. But we're not done. We're not done."

With three titles in six seasons – an achievement made more remarkable in the salary-cap era – let the talk of a dynasty begin.

"I don't know what that means," Kane said. "We've got three in six years. I know that's pretty good." ●

The party is ready to start as the Blackhawks leap over the boards after the final seconds of Game 6 expire. (John J. Kim/Chicago Tribune)

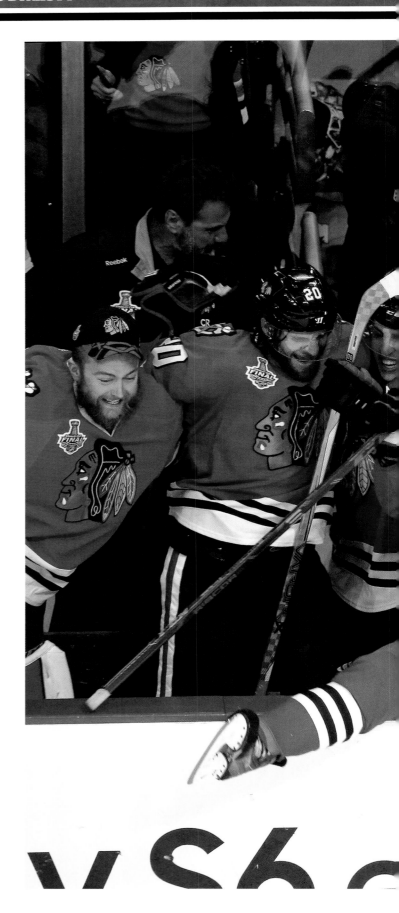

RED REIGN

Deluge can't dampen joy as Blackhawks bring home another Cup

By David Haugh

With patience wearing thin everywhere else in Chicago due to a scoreless tie at the United Center, Blackhawks star Patrick Kane waited near the blue line. And waited. Then Kane waited some more.

The Hawks had waited two years for another chance to win a Stanley Cup, what was another few seconds? Especially with Hawks defenseman Duncan Keith rushing down the ice to make the wait worthwhile.

Keith skated into the Hawks' zone and Kane patiently set up his tireless teammate with the perfect pass between two Lightning defenders. Firing a rocket that bounced off the left pad of goalie Ben Bishop, Keith followed up by knocking the rebound

past Bishop's glove at the 17-minute 13-second mark of the second period.

The horn blared, the crowd of 22,424 exhaled loudly and Chelsea Dagger played after Keith's goal that served as, well, the dagger. It only seemed fitting that the game-winner in a legacy-defining 2-0 victory over the Lightning came from Keith, who plays hockey the way teen-agers use IPhones – without worrying about the minutes that accumulate. The best player for the Hawks this postseason should be the one remembered most for winning the biggest hockey game in the city since 1938.

"Every moment is special, and this one is special because we did it in front of our fans," Keith said. "I'm just thankful and blessed. The third time winning the Cup in six years, that's unreal."

Goalie Corey Crawford shut up his critics once and for all with a shutout in a Cup-clincher. Kane, a no-show much of the series, revived "Showtime" with an insurance goal with 5 minutes 14 seconds left that started the celebration. But Keith, the unanimous Conn Smythe award winner, began a process that ended with the Hawks hoisting the silver chalice for the third time since 2010.

As Eddie Olczyk might say, threemendously threemendous.

"I think for us, we want to win almost more for those guys than for ourselves," Jonathan Toews said of the fans. "Nothing better than getting the Cup at home. It's a moment I want to be in and hold onto forever."

Once the Cup made its way through Chicago traffic to get to the arena in time for the post-game ceremony, Toews lifted above his head and exclaimed a joyful scream. Toews handed it to 40-year-old defenseman Kimmo Timonen, who will retire now. Timonen came to the Hawks via trade in March after sitting out a year with a blood clot, returning to action with the hope somehow this would happen.

"I was dreaming of this moment," Timonen said.

When Coach Joel Quenneville took his turn lifting the Cup, chants of "Q! Q!" rang out from fans who never wanted to go home. President John McDonough, a lifelong Chicagoan, understood local sentiments. The occasion marked McDonough's third Cup celebration but something about this one felt different.

"I think I'm more emotional tonight, growing up on the Northwest Side," McDonough said. "When Rocky (Wirtz) and I got together seven years ago we just wanted to get the franchise back on the right track and create a culture and build a bridge to the past … put something together that was consistent and restore the pride in being a Blackhawks fan."

Is there a fan base in all of sports prouder of its team?

In winning, the Hawks easily laid claim to the NHL's team of the decade and compelled hockey observers to spend the summer debating what constitutes a dynasty. The Red Wings also won three in the same six-year span beginning in 1997, a period in which they were coached by the legendary Scotty Bowman, now a Hawks senior advisor. His son is Stan, the Hawks general manager whose moves at the trade deadline made this third championship

possible. That father-son talk over which team enjoyed a better run would be worth crashing a summer Bowman family barbecue.

The Blackhawks under Wirtz have been a decidedly un-Chicago sports story; they warm your hearts more than they break them and win games they are supposed to win instead of letting you down for reasons analyzed for decades. They enjoy good luck created by great players, guys who generally stay out of trouble as they keep their team in contention year after year.

When the clock expired on another championship season at 9:51 p.m., everything seemed worth it – including the waiting for everyone.

What felt like the longest day of anticipation ever preceded a night that flew by, because time flies when you're having fun and this was a ball for puck fans in Chicago. At 5 p.m., the doors opened at the UC and fans sprinted down the hallways of the 300 level to claim their standing-room only seats. You would run that fast too if you spent more on a ticket than you did for rent this month. Many of the people who entered the arena wore clothes soaked by the afternoon deluge that hit the area but severe weather hardly dampened spirits. Inside, the only forecast that mattered to Hawks fans involved the Lightning leaving the area and predicting a chance for reign. It was 100 percent accurate.

One guy running by in a No. 19 sweater stopped long enough to say he paid $1,100. More than one report pegged the cost for seats in the lower level around five figures. How do you put a price on something nobody ever will forget? While their fans paid a small fortune for the experience, the Hawks dug deep looking for their championship resolve.

Unforgettably, they found it. ●

Fans reach out to greet the Blackhawks as the team takes the United Center ice for Game 6 of the Western Conference final against Anaheim. (Brian Cassella/Chicago Tribune)

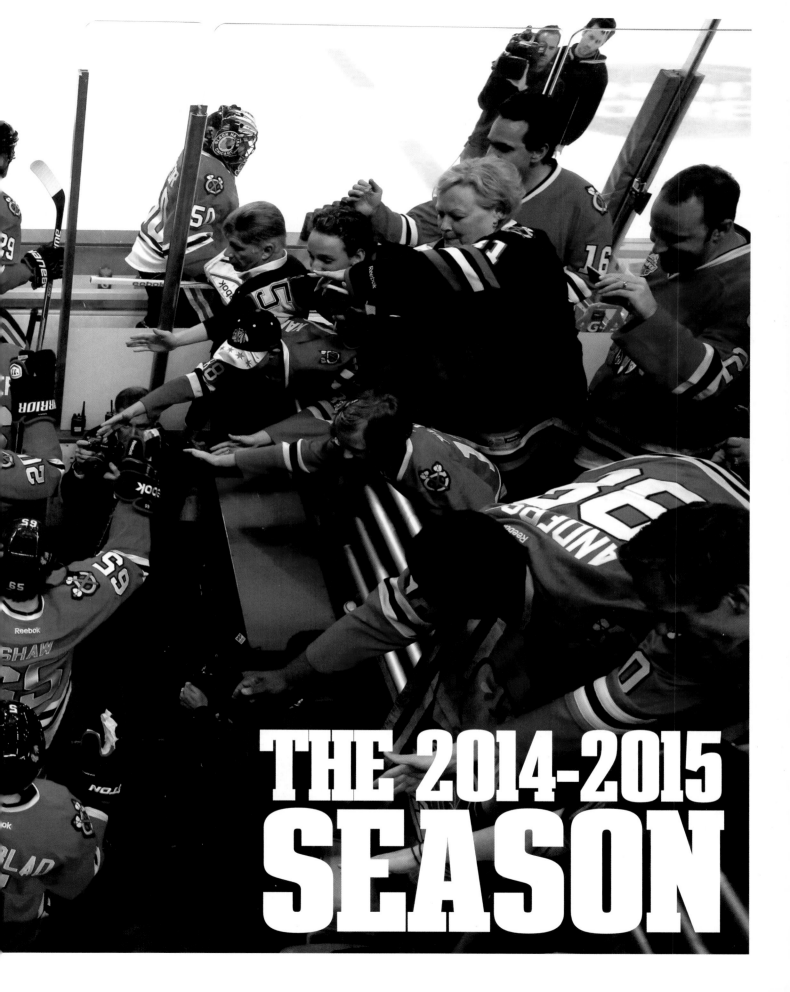

THE 2014-2015 SEASON

RIGHT WING

88
PATRICK KANE
WISE MAN

Once known as much for off-ice antics, an older,
mellowing Kane now makes news with his game

BY CHRIS KUC

Early in Patrick Kane's NHL career it seemed nary a month passed before a photo or so-called eyewitness account of the Blackhawks star enjoying himself - often a little too much - while out on the town would pop up on the Internet or light up social media.

Kane became a popular target for websites, regardless of accuracy. Some of the accounts were true – as Kane has acknowledged – and some were false.

There is no question, however, Kane was enjoying the fruits of being a young and affable professional athlete who helped resurrect one of hockey's storied franchises.

These days, the dynamic winger's exploits on the ice – and not off it – are seizing the headlines. What happened to the free spirit from Buffalo, N.Y., who at one point seemed to be on the path to jeopardizing his career with his fun-loving ways?

Kane apparently grew up.

In the summer, he surrounds himself with family and friends in his hometown and spends much of the time working out, playing in pickup hockey games and relaxing at his house that sits along a lake.

During the season when the spotlight shines brightest, Kane goes to dinner with teammates while on road trips. The next stop is usually the safe haven of his hotel room.

"Sometimes it's nice just being in your own room and having a quiet night and relaxing and getting ready for the game," Kane told the Tribune. "That's kind of where my focus is now, just trying to prepare myself as best I can and focus on the next game."

Would a 21-year-old Kane believe what the now 26-year-old Kane is saying – that life is better in the solitude of a hotel room and not in bars and nightclubs?

"No, times have changed for sure," he said. "It's

Patrick Kane learned a lesson after some of his off-ice episodes put him in an unwanted spotlight. "If you do something wrong," Kane said, "it's going to be all over the place." (Chris Sweda/Chicago Tribune)

totally different than where I used to be. I always loved the game and I always tried to do my best, but the preparation is just at a different level now."

Here's the thing about keeping a low profile in the days when everyone has a cellphone and they're not bashful to take photos or video with them: Stay on the straight and narrow and there is nothing unflattering to document.

"It's tough, but it's part of the deal these days," Kane said of being in the public eye. "One thing that has really changed is the social media with Twitter and everything. Once that came out, at the time you don't know how big it is and how much of an effect it can have on you. If you do something wrong, it's going to be all over the place. Not only does that go for me, but anyone in here. You just really have to be aware of it."

But Kane hasn't evolved into a wallflower. As one of the most recognizable sports figures in Chicago and North America and a player who is set to rake in $13.8 million next season – excluding endorsement money – he likes to have his fun. Kane is just improving on the ways he's having it.

"I feel I'm getting better for sure," he said. "I'm still 26 years old. I still feel that's fairly young. I feel like the growth has been pretty good."

Hawks coach Joel Quenneville has been around for seven of Kane's eight seasons in the NHL and agrees with that assessment.

"He has matured (more) as an individual and as a player every year," Quenneville said.

Added close friend and teammate Jonathan Toews: "He's laid back. He knows the things he needs to do to be successful and stay focused. He has learned more about himself as a person and a player."

Not coincidentally, along with Kane's growth as an individual has come a raised level of play for the Hawks. Already one of the NHL's top stars, Kane has elevated himself to the upper echelon of players this season and was a legitimate Hart Trophy candidate as the league's most valuable player before an injury cut his season short.

"He has been so consistent for us," Toews said. "Even nights when scoring is tough and maybe as a team we aren't creating much, he still finds ways to get on the board and create for our team. On the power play (or) five-on-five, it doesn't really matter. He's out there and he wants to score and he's hungry. It's great to see him playing at that level. He definitely has proven that he is one of the best in the world."

Another longtime teammate, winger Patrick Sharp, has seen Kane improve in all aspects.

"He has grown up," Sharp said. "He's very confident in himself on and off the ice. I like to mess around with Kaner and have fun with him, so I like him when he's not so mature. We can laugh and joke at the rink and make fun of each other. That's what I like best about him."

Kane's growing pains away from the game, which throughout the years included the ill-fated cab ride in Buffalo, the limo excursion in Vancouver and the Cinco de Mayo festivities in Madison, Wis., might bring some regret, but they aren't something Kane ignores.

"Everyone has their own little route," he said. "Everything that I went through made me who I am today and the player I am today."

Helping Kane along the way is a close-knit family that includes his parents, Pat Sr. and Donna,

Despite some growing pains, Patrick Kane has no regrets about how he handled his career. "Everything that I went through made me who I am today and the player I am today." (Chris Sweda/Chicago Tribune)

and sisters Erica, Jessica and Jacqueline. Just as significant is longtime girlfriend Amanda Grahovec, who has been by Kane's side for nearly three years and helps keep him grounded.

"She's great – she has helped me a lot," Kane said. "She's big into doing anything she can to help me feel better, help me be healthier, not only for my career but for longevity in life. We see a lot of each other.

When I'm home we're pretty much with each other all the time. She's a big blessing in my life for sure."

When told those sentiments sound a little like someone who might be approaching matrimony, Kane's face drained of color and he looked across the room at Toews, whom he describes as his "partner in crime," and said, "No, no. Not until after 'Tazer' does." ●

CENTER

19
JONATHAN TOEWS
HE'S ABOVE 'C' LEVEL

Hawks teammates and coaches agree,
Toews a leader in everything he does

BY CHRIS KUC

One look at Jonathan Toews racing up and down the ice with unmatched drive and determination – the "C" on his sweater standing out under the lights – makes it clear why the Blackhawks follow the example their captain sets.

During games, Toews' leadership attributes are easy to spot, but it is in moments off the ice, away from the TV cameras and adoring fans, that the 27-year-old is at his strongest as a leader.

It is Toews being the first player to raise his arms in triumph while racing across the ice to embrace an 8-year-old Make-A-Wish participant after the child scores a goal during a mid-winter practice.

It is Toews reaching out to a teammate who is struggling after the death of his closest friend and providing advice or just a shoulder to lean on.

It is conducting interviews with the media – in both English and French – while the rest of the players slip away to the team bus.

It is making sure that every teammate, even those who are scratches or just up from the minors, is made to feel he is an integral part of the group.

"That's maybe something that I've learned to step outside of my own world a little bit as I've gone along in my career," Toews said Tuesday during the 2015 Stanley Cup media day at Amalie Arena. "What makes you a successful hockey player and successful person is you're able to kind of widen your focus and understand your teammates a little bit more. To understand the dynamic of the locker room, it's no simple thing. You continue to try to learn every day. Try to understand what your teammates go through, especially some guys who are going through tough times."

A prime example of that is Toews' friendship with winger Daniel Carcillo. When the veteran was dealing

Jonathan Toews "has all the intangibles you'd like to see in a hockey player," said Blackhawks coach Joel Quenneville. "He makes people around him better." (Brian Cassella/Chicago Tribune)

with the death of best friend Steve Montador while sidelined with a concussion, it was Toews and a few other Hawks veterans who reached out with compassion to help their teammate cope with the loss.

"(Toews) has been awesome," Carcillo said. "To be able to open up to another player is hard to do, because, yeah, we see each other every day and we have that relationship, but to talk about something that you're going through, it's almost like you don't want to because you don't want to distract them or bring them down.

"He reached out and kept reaching out when I wasn't with the team (because) he knew I was going through a hard time. He's a special guy."

With all Toews has accomplished, including two Stanley Cups with the Hawks, two Olympic gold medals with Team Canada, Selke and Conn Smythe trophies – and much more – it is the respect the Winnipeg native has earned from teammates and opponents alike that best illustrates his leadership and on-ice skills.

"There are guys who lead on the ice and there are guys who lead in the dressing room – he does both," Hawks defenseman Duncan Keith said. "He's the prototypical captain that you want on your team. His demeanor and the way he cares, his passion and his commitment to hockey rubs off on not only younger guys but older guys too."

Said Hawks coach Joel Quenneville: "Will, competitive, warrior, leader – he has all the intangibles you'd like to see in a hockey player. He makes people around him better ... (and) more competitive. The way he finds ways to be successful individually and collectively is what probably makes him go better than any player."

Lightning veteran Brenden Morrow, who will skate against Toews and the Hawks during Game 1 of the Stanley Cup Final on Wednesday night, was Toews' teammate with Canada in the 2010 Olympic Winter Games in Vancouver and came away impressed.

"I don't think he has a single bad habit," Morrow said. "Winning follows him around for a good reason. He's as competitive as they come and mature beyond his years. (He's) a vocal guy, but as vocal as he is as a leader, he leads by example because his habits are so good. I can't say enough about the player he is."

After being named the third-youngest captain in NHL history in 2008 at 20, Toews has continued to grow into the role and he said he does that by observing teammates.

"My definition of being a good captain is ... to learn from the other guys in the room and what they do," he said. "We have a great group (that) understands what it means to be part of a team and give everything they have toward the common goal. We all feed off each other. A lot of guys in the room have a lot to give and I've definitely been a beneficiary of that. Win or lose, you take responsibility for it, but it's a lot of fun to be part of a group with guys like that who understand the same things." ●

Jonathan Toews was named Blackhawks captain in 2008 at age 20, making him the third youngest captain in NHL history. (Chris Sweda/Chicago Tribune)

2
DUNCAN KEITH
HAWKS' HUMBLE HERO

Keith quick to share credit, but fellow All-Stars know his true value

BY CHRIS KUC

Ask Duncan Keith to talk about himself and the defenseman quickly moves the conversation in a different direction as well as he steers opposing forwards away from the Blackhawks net.

"I can talk about myself," Keith said during 2015 NHL All-Star Game festivities at Nationwide Arena in Columbus. "A lot of my success is through my hard work and through my determination."

OK, now we're getting somewhere.

"But I know a lot of it is a credit to my teammates," Keith said. "It's fun being a part of a team like this and an organization like this. I don't think you get honors without being surrounded by great players."

See?

Participating in the All-Star Game – Keith's third to go along with two Norris trophies as the league's best defenseman and two Olympic gold medals with Team Canada – the 31-year-old Winnipeg native is surrounded by the top players in the NHL.

Unlike Keith, they aren't reluctant to talk about Keith.

"He's someone who I like to try to play like," said the Blues' Kevin Shattenkirk. "I don't want to say he's reckless but he jumps into the rush and he's very confident in his skating abilities to recover and get back. What impresses me the most is his ability to, at the right time, find a scoring opportunity and make it count. He's someone who can be very dangerous when he's playing his best and can really make you pay."

Added Predators defenseman Shea Weber, a five-time NHL All-Star: "What's not to like? He does everything. He's such a complete defenseman. He skates so well, sees the ice so he's able to do the things he wants offensively and shuts guys down defensively. A lot of people would love to play with him."

The Kings' Drew Doughty knows Keith's game well, having been his defensive partner during the 2010 Olympics in Vancouver in addition to battles during the regular season and playoffs.

"I love Duncan's game – he's a fantastic player," Doughty said. "He plays well defensively and he plays well offensively. He's a just a complete defenseman. He's not physical, too, which is kind of cool because he's able to play so well defensively. With myself, to play well defensively I have to be physical and he finds a way to not have to do it. He's just so smart with his

A second-round pick out of Michigan State University in 2002, Duncan Keith has become one of the premier defensemen in the NHL. (Brian Cassella/Chicago Tribune)

stick and so fast with his feet, he turns pucks over that way. He's without a doubt one of the best defensemen in this league."

It is Keith's consistency that draws the most admiration from opponents.

"He's a pro," Wild defenseman Ryan Suter said. "He doesn't have a bad game. What has made him so good is you know what you're going to get from him every night and it's going to be a good, solid 60-minute game."

Fellow defensemen aren't the only experts on the subject of Keith. The forwards around the league who have gotten their fill while trying to solve him wax poetically about the veteran.

"It's not so much when he's in front of you, it's when you're chasing him up the ice that's the hard mindset," Ducks center Ryan Getzlaf said. "Duncan is a player you have to keep in front of you all the time. He does an unbelievable job of getting up and down the rink in a hurry and forcing you into situations that you don't want to be in."

Said Oilers center Ryan Nugent-Hopkins: "He's a tough guy to beat, he's so mobile. He's a really smart player so you just have to try to chip it by. He's fast, too, so you can't really let up. When you're back-checking on him you have to really be aware that he's going to take off." ●

LEFT WING

20
BRANDON SAAD
SAAD'S SQUAD

With assist from family,
young star reaches goal

BY CHRIS KUC

That Brandon Saad's journey to the NHL began with ball hockey games in the cul-de-sac in front of his childhood home in Gibsonia, Pa., is telling.

Family is entwined through the fabric of Saad's progression from natural athlete growing up in the community about 25 miles north of Pittsburgh to Blackhawks left wing with a future as bright as any young player in the NHL.

At 22, he has already earned the faith of coach Joel Quenneville, having played a huge role in the Hawks' run to the 2013 Stanley Cup and is an integral part of the current group. Once the playoffs end, Saad will become a restricted free agent, one who could tempt other teams to tender him an offer sheet. But general manager Stan Bowman leaves little room for doubt about Saad's future.

"He's emerged as a guy coaches trust, so I would think he's going to play an even bigger role next year," Bowman told the Tribune. "He's ready for that. He'll be 23 and he'll have a couple of years of solid NHL experience under his belt. He's ready for taking that next step to being a featured guy.

"We'll get him signed."

Saad's odyssey to reach this point has ties that run from Syria to Pennsylvania to Chicago.

It is a tale that includes a grandfather who was an NFL official who worked two Super Bowls, a father who moved to the United States from Syria at 18 and continues to work to bring every relative still in the war-torn country to safety in the United States, a stay-at-home mother who introduced her two sons to hockey and a brother who was a standout player and mentor before injuries derailed his career.

They helped Saad develop from a boy who collected hundreds of hockey pucks that he kept

At age 22, Brandon Saad set a career high in 2014-15 with 23 goals, including six game-winners. As a kid growing up in Pittsburgh, Saad originally wanted to be a goalie. (Nuccio DiNuzzo/Chicago Tribune)

under his bed and at one point told teachers he didn't need to study "because I'm going to be a hockey player someday" to the top line of the Hawks.

"We were always close growing up, whether it was my parents or brother doing sports together and my parents working to provide for us," Saad said. "They are the reason I'm here today."

It was those countless hockey games on roller blades against friends and brother George Saad Jr. that kicked things off.

"In the street, we always played against each other," Brandon said of his older brother. "Being a couple of years older, he was always a little bigger, a little stronger and faster, and that helped me with trying to compete with the big boys. It helped me elevate my game."

First, though, mother Sandra had to step in and make an adjustment.

"Brandon always wanted to be a goalie," she said. "I said, 'Son, you can't be there, you have too much speed, so don't think about it.'"

Saad's speed, natural ability and drive became apparent early on.

"He never liked to lose," George Jr. said. "Being brothers we always battled it out and pushed each other. He always was very driven. If he did lose, he always wanted to keep playing until he won. He always gave his best to be the best he could be."

Hockey wasn't always the family sport.

"I grew up with football," Sandra said.

Her father, Gil Mace, was an NFL official, who worked Super Bowl XVIII in 1984 as a back judge and Super Bowl XXI in 1987 as a side judge.

Brandon and his brother played hockey and football in high school but eventually had to make a

decision, and hockey won out. They played together in junior hockey before George Jr. headed off to Penn State.

"I played a lot of sports growing up, just trying to be a well-rounded athlete and then when I got to high school I just focused on hockey," Brandon said. "I've always seemed to have success at it and always had more fun playing it. I love the speed of the game."

Saad eventually landed in the U.S. National Team Development Program, where he caught Bowman's eye as a non-draft-eligible underage player.

"When I went to watch the U.S. program, they said the best forwards on this team are the underages and this kid here, Saad, is going to be a great player," Bowman said. "He was skilled, but he wasn't like Patrick Kane. He wasn't dazzling, he just was effective. He did the right things all the time. He's strong and he just knew how to play the game."

The Hawks selected Saad in the second round of the 2011 NHL draft, and two years later he was skating on the top line with Jonathan Toews and Marian Hossa, helping lead the Hawks to their second Stanley Cup in four years.

"(Saad) is a powerful guy," Bowman said. "When you play with two elite players like Toews and Hossa, those guys are superstars, so for a young kid to come in and be able to read off them and be able to complement them to the point where they enjoy playing with him? That says something. They enjoyed playing with him from the first time that line came together. It's his recognition, his ability to instinctively know how they're going to play."

Saad took a big step during the 2014-15 season, setting career highs with 23 goals – including six game-winners – 29 assists and 52 points. He also played a big role in the Hawks' playoff run – including a key short-handed score during the 5-4 victory over the Ducks in Game 4 of the Western Conference final.

"He's going to be a big part of our team going forward," Bowman said.

One potential hurdle is another team submitting an offer sheer for Saad that the Hawks would have to match. A big offer could deepen the Hawks' salary-cap woes, but Bowman said he isn't concerned.

Neither is Saad.

"I want to end up in Chicago for sure," he said. "They've treated me nothing but great here."

Whatever his future holds, Saad's family will continue to be by his side. His biggest fans are his parents, led by his hockey-crazed father, George Sr., who grew up in Syria, not exactly a hockey hotbed.

"I had absolutely zero exposure to hockey," George Sr. said. "Now, I am actually as fanatic as you're going to get. The whole family follows him: cousins, aunts, uncles – they're hooked."

Among those are the family members the land developer has brought to the U.S. from Syria, which is in the throes of a civil war.

"Most of my family is in the States," George Sr. said. "We're Christians, and the Christian families in Syria unfortunately have been killed and slaughtered. We had to sponsor them to avoid persecution. There are a couple of more sisters that I'm going to bring in the next couple of months with their families. They're learning the language, (and) they're improving in school. They're fitting into the culture nicely."

Brandon Saad has followed the developments even while focusing on hockey.

"We're getting most of them to come over here and live near us and become American citizens," he

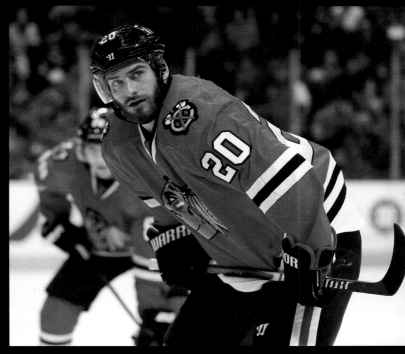

Just two years after he was taken in the second round of the 2011 draft, Brandon Saad was playing on the top line for the Stanley Cup champion Blackhawks. (Nuccio DiNuzzo/Chicago Tribune)

said. "It's been great hearing stories about that. Any day with stuff going on there anything can happen, but for the majority they're all safe and it feels good."

That is important to Saad, who credits his upbringing and continued closeness with his family for his success.

"That's a huge part of it to have that support," he said. "All of us want to be here, but to have that drive and have that support behind you is always huge. For me, personally, it's why I'm here." ●

GOALTENDER

50
COREY CRAWFORD
IN HIS COMFORT ZONE

Blackhawks goalie raising his
game to earlier heights

BY CHRIS KUC

If his 300-plus games in the NHL have taught Corey Crawford anything, it's to live in the here and now. The Blackhawks goaltender learns from the past, moves on and makes it a point to never look too far ahead.

"There's one game – there's tomorrow," Crawford said. "You can tire yourself out mentally when you start thinking about how many games are left. Or you look at the standings and you start thinking too much. Then too much is on your mind and maybe you're not 100 percent focused on what you have to do on the ice."

After being one of the NHL's top goalies for the first two months of the season, Crawford injured his left ankle while attending a concert in Chicago. In the immediate aftermath of the eight games he missed in December, Crawford was inconsistent and the Hawks followed suit.

"You always have to adjust when you come back from an injury with timing and picking up shots off the stick," he said. "I thought I picked it up fairly quickly, but I just wasn't getting results right away."

At 30, Crawford has reached a point in his career where his knowledge of the game has caught up to his talent. His progression took a giant step after the 2011-12 season during which he posted the highest goals-against average (2.72) and lowest save percentage (.903) of his career.

"You learn a lot throughout the years, especially my second year I learned a lot," Crawford said. "I was maybe getting down on myself a little bit more than I should have, which was kind of affecting the games. It would kind of last for stretches too. After playing a bunch of years I think you realize you just have to keep playing hard and don't let anything affect you.

"You have to adapt and just everything comes together. It's about preparing the same way, preparing to be at your best so you don't have those off days."

Coach Joel Quenneville has seen Crawford's evolution both physically and mentally, especially under the guidance of goaltending coach Jimmy Waite.

"Goalies, they learn a lot," Quenneville said. "They learn about themselves, they learn about the

After missing eight games with an ankle injury in December, Corey Crawford had to work his way back into the form that made him one of the NHL's top goaltenders. (Chris Sweda/Chicago Tribune)

league, shots (and) the defense in front of them. 'Crow' is a smart kid. He's adapting well and absorbing any information he can. He computes it and handles it the right way as far as taking advantage of the next situation. Preparation for goaltenders to me is everything. Jimmy does a real nice job with him as far as the focus and getting himself excited for the next challenge. Crow is definitely improving in that area."

The teammates who have been along for the ride believe Crawford has reached the upper echelon of goaltenders.

"I think he's flying a little bit under the radar when it comes to being one of the best goalies in the league," defenseman Niklas Hjalmarsson said. "It's not very often you see him let in an easy goal. You usually have to beat him pretty good to be able to score so he's been one of our best players the whole season. He's been steady as a rock." ●

Learning how to cope with defeats was an important step for Corey Crawford. "I was maybe getting down on myself a little more than I should have," the Hawks goalie said. (Chris Sweda/Chicago Tribune)

SO CLOSE THEY STILL TASTE IT

Hawks vow to use last season's bitter end as motivation to win back the Stanley Cup

By Chris Kuc

ONE GOAL.

It's not just a marketing slogan, it's also what kept the Blackhawks from cementing their legacy as an NHL dynasty.

Not all losses are created equal and Exhibit A was the Hawks' gut-wrenching 5-4 overtime defeat to the Kings in Game 7 of the Western Conference finals last season. The Alec Martinez shot that deflected off then-Hawks defenseman Nick Leddy twice and wobbled into the net denied the Hawks a berth in the Stanley Cup Final against the Rangers, ending their bid for back-to-back championships and three in five years.

It wasn't just another loss for Hawks players; it was the toughest many ever had experienced.

"When you think what kind of team we had and how close we were to getting to the finals, it definitely was the worst loss in my career and a lot of guys' careers," winger Bryan Bickell said. "One shot or bounce and we could have been back to the finals."

The loss still resonates in the dressing room as the Hawks regroup and prepare for the season that kicks off against the Stars in Dallas. The opener will serve as a chance to begin to erase the memory of what could have been. A summer separated from the shockingly abrupt ending helped ease the pain, but it's a wound that may never heal fully until the Hawks again hoist the Cup.

"Everyone between the third period and overtime had that feeling we were going to go back to the finals, so it was a pretty heartbreaking loss," goaltender Corey Crawford said. "It's a tough league. It's tough to win a Stanley Cup and it's even tougher to win two in a row."

Instead of attempting to tuck it into the dark recesses of their psyche, the Hawks will use the feelings of disappointment as fuel.

"With all those good times we had when we

No strangers to the spotlight, the Blackhawks are introduced before the season opener on Oct. 11, 2014 at the United Center, their first game since a crushing overtime loss to the Kings in Game 7 of the Western Conference final four months earlier. (Nuccio DiNuzzo/Chicago Tribune)

won in 2013 that we had taken away from us last year, everyone wants to experience that again and have those celebrations and lift that Cup again," Crawford said.

That desire to climb back to the top starts in the upper echelon of the organization and filters down.

"There's an incredible hunger," President John McDonough said. "This team has a bit of a chip on its shoulder. Hey, we're the underdog. We always have something to prove."

Said captain Jonathan Toews: "It's just motivation knowing the potential and knowing how close we came and understanding that we're going to be even better having learned from that experience and using that as a source of energy to improve upon.

"You can dwell on the other things like having gone through two really, really good teams to get there and passing up the opportunity ... but to a certain extent it's remembering that moment and how hurtful it was but also turning the page and moving on to this year.

"We know it can be a special year if we put everything together and we find a way to improve every single day. We can't fast forward to that seventh game in the conference final right now, but obviously that's on our minds and will be as we go through this season." ●

The Blackhawks entered the 2014-15 season as one of the favorites to win the Stanley Cup. "We know it can be a special year," said Hawks captain Jonathan Toews. (Nuccio DiNuzzo/Chicago Tribune)

GOSSIP GONE WILD CROSSES THE LINE

Salacious rumors on Internet take toll on Sharp

By David Haugh

Blackhawks forward Patrick Sharp decided enough was enough.

His parents had called with questions. His in-laws did, too, along with other family members and friends. At a charity function thrown by teammate Bryan Bickell, Sharp privately stewed unable to escape the reach of the rumormongering. A website that promotes itself as the home of "Chicago Sports News, Rumors & Gossip" posted an uncomfortably detailed list of Sharp's alleged infidelities and incidents with teammates while speculating the Blackhawks had suffered as a result. It was the cyber equivalent of a cross-check into the boards and, shaken, Sharp revealed he plans to consult an attorney about potential legal action.

"It's been tough," Sharp said. "As a hockey player, as a professional, you're out there and you're up for grabs for on-ice play. I'm OK with that. But when people delve into your personal life, make up rumors and things that are completely false and untrue, it takes a toll on you, your family, your friends, and it's completely unnecessary."

It is one thing for somebody covering the Blackhawks to vaguely attribute Sharp's struggles to personal problems – he would be far from the first professional athlete to let issues at home affect him on the job. It is another to publish salacious allegations without proof or attribution in a manner that crosses the lines of journalistic fairness, regardless of whether Sharp qualifies as a public figure.

The Hawks have become rock stars in Chicago, but limits still exist for how far we should be entitled to pry into their lives. Sharp never addressed the website's specific allegations Sunday because, thankfully, nobody asked. It's none of our business.

"It's unbelievable – it has nothing to do with my job," Sharp said of the gossip. "I don't know where it gets started or how it snowballs. I wish I could say it's all rolling off my back. Part of it is. But when you continue to hear stuff about you, sooner or later you have to defend yourself."

So Sharp removed his equipment, stared into the cameras and attempted to do just that. His voice quivered at times and he sounded more hurt than

Patrick Sharp cradles daughter Sadie while chatting with teammate Andrew Shaw during a holiday event at the United Center in December, 2014. During the season, Sharp became the subject of numerous rumors regarding his life off the ice. (Michael Tercha/Chicago Tribune)

angry. This wasn't Patrick Sharp the picture of debonair we are used to seeing handle everything smoothly. This was a troubled 33-year-old father and husband trying to deal with a private crisis publicly, worrying what he will tell his two young daughters about all this one day.

"They're ages 3 and 1, but when you think about if they ever will hear about this kind of stuff (later), it breaks your heart," Sharp said. "I talk to other people about it and they say, 'Oh, my God, it's hilarious, don't even worry about it.' I wish I could do that. I can't. You can see how much it affects me."

"Obviously, it was bothering him, but we're working our way through it as a team," coach Joel Quenneville said. ●

BLACKHAWKS

STAR STRUCK

Cup bid takes big hit: Kane out 12 weeks with fractured collarbone

By Chris Kuc

Kris Versteeg called Patrick Kane "irreplaceable."

So how do the Blackhawks go about replacing the irreplaceable?

"That's a good question," winger Patrick Sharp said. And the Hawks need a good answer after Kane had surgery to repair a fractured left collarbone suffered Feb. 24 against the Panthers. He will be sidelined approximately 12 weeks.

Kane, 26, was placed on long-term injured reserve and likely will return this season only if the Hawks can make a deep run in the Stanley Cup playoffs.

Teuvo Teravainen was recalled from Rockford to fill Kane's roster spot, but the rookie won't be counted on solely to fill Kane's scoring role.

Before the injury, Kane was tied for the NHL scoring lead with 27 goals and 37 assists, and the Hawks will look to fill the void by committee and defensive structure.

"You have the leading scorer in the game, a very valuable asset. He makes a lot of things work for us," coach Joel Quenneville said of Kane, who suffered the injury when he fell awkwardly into the boards after a cross-check from the Panthers' Alex Petrovic in the first period of a Hawks' 3-2 shootout victory.

"As a group, we have to make sure everybody plays the right way, plays tighter and has some responsibility to their games. We have to play tight and look to play low-scoring games."

General manager Stan Bowman also could seek to bolster the lineup via trade. In the meantime, the Hawks' recalled Teravainen, activated Trevor van Riemsdyk from long-term IR and then sent the rookie defenseman to Rockford. They also placed Kane on IR, a series of moves that opened up roughly $6 million of salary-cap space.

Meanwhile, the worst-case scenario for the Hawks regarding the time Kane will miss is a significant blow to the chances – and psyche – of a team with Stanley Cup aspirations.

"I can't count the number of times Kaner has missed a shift on one hand in his career let alone not return to the game," Sharp said. "He brings so much to our team. He's having a great season individually and he makes us a better team in a lot of areas."

The Hawks now must regroup for the final 21 games of the regular season.

"It's just another blow," Sharp said. "It happens every season, whether it's injuries, losing streaks, you name it. It's just another obstacle to climb." ●

After he fractured his left collarbone on February 24, 2015, Patrick Kane was expected to be out of action for up to 12 weeks. (Chris Sweda/Chicago Tribune)

DEADLINE DEALS SHOW IT'S ALL ABOUT NOW

Chance for a Cup outweighs losing future draft pick

By Chris Kuc

Ben Smith didn't waste any time departing the United Center and getting on a plane headed to San Jose after he became the only rostered player dealt by the Blackhawks before the NHL trade deadline.

General manager Stan Bowman did what he set out to do, bringing in key pieces while keeping the Hawks roster relatively intact.

In the days leading up to the deadline, Bowman added Antoine Vermette and Kimmo Timonen and then acquired Andrew Desjardins from the Sharks. To land the veterans, Bowman mortgaged some of the future. In addition to giving up the 26-year-old Smith, the Hawks traded prospect Klas Dahlbeck, 23, and four draft picks, including first- and second-rounders this year, a conditional fourth in '16 and a conditional seventh in '17.

"We obviously like the group here," Bowman said. "They've accomplished a lot as a group. You're trying to give them a boost and add to the group.

"You have to pay a price, obviously, giving up some prospects and draft picks, but that's where the organization strength comes in," Bowman added. "You don't like to give up draft picks, but at the same time, it is a draft pick – you have time to recoup those down the road. Right now, we're trying to improve our team. I think we have a good chance to be even better than we've been. We (brought in) three new faces to give our group some excitement and push for the playoffs."

All three newcomers are considered rental players as they have expiring contracts, something crucial for the Hawks when they will go to assemble next season's roster and will need every cent they can get under the NHL's salary cap.

Still, Bowman did not rule out the return of Vermette or Desjardins. Timonen has said he will retire after this season.

"Whenever we acquire players, we want to see how they fit in," Bowman said. "The same thing happened a couple years ago. We added Johnny Oduya (in 2012) and he was such a great fit that we made it a priority to bring him back. ... We'll have an offseason puzzle to put together and we don't have

Andrew Desjardins was one of three veterans the Blackhawks acquired before the trade deadline in an attempt to shore up their depth for a long playoff run. (Chris Sweda/Chicago Tribune)

to solve that one now. But we'd be very interested in trying to keep going if it works."

The departure of the popular Smith – a member of the 2013 Cup winners – was a blow to the Hawks' dressing room perhaps more than on the ice, but the team was happy no one else had to leave a group that had battled together for 63 games this season.

"Anytime somebody gets traded it's tough,"

defenseman Duncan Keith said. "There are guys who you're closer with than other guys. Maybe you've played with them longer and developed more of a bond. At the same time, nothing changes in the way that you're still on the same team and anytime somebody goes to another team you know they've already become the enemy. It's just sports. That's the tough part." ●

KANE MAKES HAWKS WHOLE

Winger's return should provide boost to offense

By Chris Hine

A small smile flashed across Patrick Kane's face when he was asked if he was going to play in Game 1 of the Hawks' playoff series against the Predators.

"Yeah, that's the plan," Kane said.

And with that, the speculation was over.

The Hawks will officially welcome back one of the league's dynamic scorers and playoff producers as Kane beat the initial 12-week timetable to rehab the broken left collarbone he suffered Feb. 24.

"It's been a long 50 days here, so it's a credit to a lot of hard work from obviously the doctors and the trainers and just listening to them and trying to heal as fast as possible," Kane said.

To do that, Kane said the team tried a few rehabilitation techniques but declined to describe them.

Kane showed progress in recent weeks during practice and took contact for the first time Monday before team doctors fully cleared him.

"There's definitely three or four different things that we tried and seemed to work," Kane said. "It seemed to just improve week by week. So we're at the point right now where it's pretty safe to go out there and try and compete and play."

Coach Joel Quenneville and captain Jonathan Toews flashed similar subtle smiles to Kane's on Tuesday when asked about Kane's return.

"For a while there no one was too sure how long the recovery period would take for him," Toews said. "So obviously it's good news that he feels ready to go."

Quenneville said in February he did not think it would be possible for Kane to return to the lineup this quickly.

"It wasn't in the cards knowing we had to get through a round or two before he could even be considered," Quenneville said. "This is a very positive situation for us, knowing what he brings to the table. He was having an MVP type of season."

Kane is no stranger to beginning the playoffs after an extended break. Last season, he didn't play for nearly a month as he rested an injured knee before taking the ice in the first round against the Blues. Kane ended up scoring nine goals and 10 assists in 23 games.

"Last year in the playoffs, it seemed like I started a little slow and then kind of picked it up as the playoffs went on," Kane said. "So I think you can learn from that." ●

Patrick Kane's early return from a collarbone injury gave the Blackhawks a huge boost heading into the first round of the playoffs. (Antonio Perez/Chicago Tribune)

2014-15 BLACKHAWKS GAME-BY-GAME RESULTS

GP	DATE	OPPONENT	RES	OT/SO	HAWKS	OPP	W	L	OL	STREAK
1	10/9/14	@ Dallas Stars	W	SO	3	2	1	0	0	W 1
2	10/11/14	Buffalo Sabres	W		6	2	2	0	0	W 2
3	10/15/14	Calgary Flames	L	OT	1	2	2	0	1	L 1
4	10/18/14	Nashville Predators	W	OT	2	1	3	0	1	W 1
5	10/21/14	Philadelphia Flyers	W		4	0	4	0	1	W 2
6	10/23/14	@ Nashville Predators	L		2	3	4	1	1	L 1
7	10/25/14	@ St. Louis Blues	L		2	3	4	2	1	L 2
8	10/26/14	Ottawa Senators	W		2	1	5	2	1	W 1
9	10/28/14	Anaheim Ducks	L		0	1	5	3	1	L 1
10	10/30/14	@ Ottawa Senators	W	SO	5	4	6	3	1	W 1

GP	DATE	OPPONENT	RES	OT/SO	HAWKS	OPP	W	L	OL	STREAK
11	11/1/14	@ Toronto Maple Leafs	L		2	3	6	4	1	L 1
12	11/2/14	Winnipeg Jets	L		0	1	6	5	1	L 2
13	11/4/14	@ Montreal Canadiens	W		5	0	7	5	1	W 1
14	11/7/14	Washington Capitals	L		2	3	7	6	1	L 1
15	11/9/14	San Jose Sharks	W		5	2	8	6	1	W 1
16	11/11/14	Tampa Bay Lightning	W	SO	3	2	9	6	1	W 2
17	11/14/14	@ Detroit Red Wings	L		1	4	9	7	1	L 1
18	11/16/14	Dallas Stars	W		6	2	10	7	1	W 1
19	11/20/14	@ Calgary Flames	W		4	3	11	7	1	W 2
20	11/22/14	@ Edmonton Oilers	W		7	1	12	7	1	W 3
21	11/23/14	@ Vancouver Canucks	L		1	4	12	8	1	L 1
22	11/26/14	@ Colorado Avalanche	W		3	2	13	8	1	W 1
23	11/28/14	@ Anaheim Ducks	W		4	1	14	8	1	W 2
24	11/29/14	@ Los Angeles Kings	W		4	1	15	8	1	W 3

GP	DATE	OPPONENT	RES	OT/SO	HAWKS	OPP	W	L	OL	STREAK
25	12/3/14	St. Louis Blues	W		4	1	16	8	1	W 4
26	12/5/14	Montreal Canadiens	W		4	3	17	8	1	W 5
27	12/6/14	@ Nashville Predators	W		3	1	18	8	1	W 6
28	12/9/14	@ New Jersey Devils	W	SO	3	2	19	8	1	W 7
29	12/11/14	@ Boston Bruins	W		3	2	20	8	1	W 8
30	12/13/14	@ New York Islanders	L		2	3	20	9	1	L 1
31	12/14/14	Calgary Flames	W		2	1	21	9	1	W 1
32	12/16/14	Minnesota Wild	W		5	3	22	9	1	W 2
33	12/20/14	@ Columbus Blue Jackets	L	SO	2	3	22	9	2	L 1
34	12/21/14	Toronto Maple Leafs	W		4	0	23	9	2	W 1
35	12/23/14	Winnipeg Jets	L		1	5	23	10	2	L 1
36	12/27/14	@ Colorado Avalanche	W		5	2	24	10	2	W 1
37	12/29/14	Nashville Predators	W	SO	5	4	25	10	2	W 2

GP	DATE	OPPONENT	RES	OT/SO	HAWKS	OPP	W	L	OL	STREAK
38	1/1/15	@ Washington Capitals	L		2	3	25	11	2	L 1
39	1/4/15	Dallas Stars	W	OT	5	4	26	11	2	W 1
40	1/6/15	Colorado Avalanche	L		0	2	26	12	2	L 1
41	1/8/15	@ Minnesota Wild	W		4	2	27	12	2	W 1
42	1/9/15	@ Edmonton Oilers	L		2	5	27	13	2	L 1
43	1/11/15	Minnesota Wild	W		4	1	28	13	2	W 1
44	1/16/15	Winnipeg Jets	L		2	4	28	14	2	L 1
45	1/18/15	Dallas Stars	L		3	6	28	15	2	L 2
46	1/20/15	Arizona Coyotes	W		6	1	29	15	2	W 1
47	1/21/15	@ Pittsburgh Penguins	W	SO	3	2	30	15	2	W 2
48	1/28/15	@ Los Angeles Kings	L		3	4	30	16	2	L 1
49	1/30/15	@ Anaheim Ducks	W		4	1	31	16	2	W 1
50	1/31/15	@ San Jose Sharks	L		0	2	31	17	2	L 1

GP	DATE	OPPONENT	RES	OT/SO	HAWKS	OPP	W	L	OL	STREAK
51	2/3/15	@ Minnesota Wild	L		0	3	31	18	2	L 2
52	2/6/15	@ Winnipeg Jets	W	OT	2	1	32	18	2	W 1
53	2/8/15	@ St. Louis Blues	W		4	2	33	18	2	W 2
54	2/9/15	Arizona Coyotes	L	SO	2	3	33	18	3	L 1
55	2/11/15	Vancouver Canucks	L	OT	4	5	33	18	4	L 2
56	2/13/15	New Jersey Devils	W		3	1	34	18	4	W 1
57	2/15/15	Pittsburgh Penguins	W	SO	2	1	35	18	4	W 2
58	2/18/15	Detroit Red Wings	L	SO	2	3	35	18	5	L 1
59	2/20/15	Colorado Avalanche	L		1	4	35	19	5	L 2
60	2/22/15	Boston Bruins	L		2	6	35	20	5	L 3
61	2/24/15	Florida Panthers	W	SO	3	2	36	20	5	W 1
62	2/26/15	@ Florida Panthers	W		3	0	37	20	5	W 2
63	2/27/15	@ Tampa Bay Lightning	L		0	4	37	21	5	L 1

GP	DATE	OPPONENT	RES	OT/SO	HAWKS	OPP	W	L	OL	STREAK
64	3/2/15	Carolina Hurricanes	W		5	2	38	21	5	W 1
65	3/6/15	Edmonton Oilers	W	SO	2	1	39	21	5	W 2
66	3/8/15	New York Rangers	L	OT	0	1	39	21	6	L 1
67	3/12/15	@ Arizona Coyotes	W		2	1	40	21	6	W 1
68	3/14/15	@ San Jose Sharks	W		6	2	41	21	6	W 2
69	3/17/15	New York Islanders	W		4	1	42	21	6	W 3
70	3/18/15	@ New York Rangers	W		1	0	43	21	6	W 4
71	3/21/15	@ Dallas Stars	L		0	4	43	22	6	L 1
72	3/23/15	@ Carolina Hurricanes	W		3	1	44	22	6	W 1
73	3/25/15	@ Philadelphia Flyers	L		1	4	44	23	6	L 1
74	3/27/15	Columbus Blue Jackets	L		2	5	44	24	6	L 2
75	3/29/15	@ Winnipeg Jets	W		4	3	45	24	6	W 1
76	3/30/15	Los Angeles Kings	W		4	1	46	24	6	W 2

GP	DATE	OPPONENT	RES	OT/SO	HAWKS	OPP	W	L	OL	STREAK
77	4/2/15	Vancouver Canucks	W		3	1	47	24	6	W 3
78	4/3/15	@ Buffalo Sabres	W		4	3	48	24	6	W 4
79	4/5/15	St. Louis Blues	L		1	2	48	25	6	L 1
80	4/7/15	Minnesota Wild	L		1	2	48	26	6	L 2
81	4/9/15	@ St. Louis Blues	L		1	2	48	27	6	L 3
82	4/11/15	@ Colorado Avalanche	L		2	3	48	28	6	L 4

FIRST ROUND 4-2 OVER THE PREDATORS

After Hawks goaltender Corey Crawford allowed three goals in the first period of Game 1, coach Joel Quenneville turned to Scott Darling, who made 42 saves as the Hawks came back to win in double overtime. After Crawford struggled again in a Game 2 loss, Darling took over for Games 3, 4, and 5 and guided the Hawks to a 3-2 series lead. The Hawks won a triple-overtime thriller in Game 4. The goaltending situation came full circle when Crawford replaced Darling in Game 6 after Darling allowed three first-period goals. The Hawks won the clincher 4-3, and Crawford would not leave the net again in the postseason.

GAME 1: HAWKS 4, PREDATORS 3 (2OT)
GAME 2: PREDATORS 6, HAWKS 2
GAME 3: HAWKS 4, PREDATORS 2
GAME 4: HAWKS 3, PREDATORS 2 (3OT)
GAME 5: PREDATORS 5, HAWKS 2
GAME 6: HAWKS 4, PREDATORS 3

Backup goalie Scott Darling was the unlikely hero for the Blackhawks in Round 1 of the playoffs, winning three games in the series. (Nuccio DiNuzzo/Chicago Tribune)

WESTERN CONFERENCE QUARTERFINALS

Game 1

April 15, 2015

Blackhawks 4, Predators 3 (2OT)

OH, DARLING!

Backup goalie perfect in relief after Crawford gets the early hook
Keith's goal in 2nd overtime caps thrilling rally from 3-goal deficit

By Chris Kuc

On the list of potential heroes for the Blackhawks in Game 1 of their first-round playoff series against the Predators, Scott Darling ranked just above the assistant coaches.

Yet it was the rookie from Lemont who was absolutely brilliant in relief of starting goaltender Corey Crawford, propelling the Hawks to an improbable 4-3 double-overtime victory over the Predators at Bridgestone Arena.

After Crawford yielded three goals that had his team down and nearly out, Darling entered the game to start the second period and made 42 saves - many of them spectacular - as the Hawks seized home-ice advantage in the best-of-seven series.

"This is just another thing that I never would have told you would have happened, but it did," Darling said.

Duncan Keith scored the winner 7 minutes, 49 seconds into the second OT, capping a comeback from a three-goal deficit after one period of ragged defensive play.

With the help of two assists from by Patrick Kane,

playing in his first game since suffering a broken left collarbone Feb. 24, the Hawks roared back in the second on goals from Jonathan Toews, Patrick Sharp and Niklas Hjalmarsson. Those goals negated two from Colin Wilson and another from Viktor Stalberg that had the crowd roaring and the Hawks on their heels in the opening period.

From there, Darling and Pekka Rinne engaged in a classic goalie duel, but when the dust settled it was Darling still standing.

"It was a great opportunity for (Darling) and he seized the moment," Hawks coach Joel Quenneville said. "Playing in a playoff game of this magnitude in that situation it was one of the greatest relief performances you're going to see."

Kane logged 23:08 in his return and looked dangerous with the puck after a shaky first period.

"I felt a little rusty," Kane said. "It's nothing I didn't really expect after some time off and coming back for the first playoff game. It was good for me to get a game under my belt and even better that we got the win. Hopefully, I keep improving." ●

Scott Darling goes into the snow-angel position to make a save during the Blackhawks 4-3 overtime victory over Nashville in the playoff opener. (Nuccio DiNuzzo/Chicago Tribune)

Game 2
April 17, 2015
Predators 6, Blackhawks 2

RICKETY SPLIT

In shaky 3rd, Predators turn up heat to even series

By Chris Kuc

They arrived in Nashville looking for one victory and once they got it, the Blackhawks got greedy.

And why not? Taking a 2-0 lead on the road in a best-of-seven series goes a long way toward a short postseason round.

"We came here to try to grab at least one victory and we already have the first one, which was really, really important," winger Marian Hossa said before the Hawks took the ice against the Predators in Game 2 of the first-round series at Bridgestone Arena. "Now, we would like to get another one."

They didn't.

The Predators got goals by Craig Smith, Colin Wilson and Roman Josi in the first two periods and then blew the game open in the second half of the third with goals from Filip Forsberg, Wilson and Mike Santorelli to post a 6-2 victory over the Hawks behind strong goaltending from Pekka Rinne. The triumph evened the series at one game apiece with Game 3 at the United Center.

Patrick Sharp and Patrick Kane scored for the Hawks, but it wasn't enough as Corey Crawford suffered the loss in goal. The Predators' victory was that much more impressive as they played without captain Shea Weber for the second half of the game after the defenseman suffered a lower-body injury.

It was another close postseason game, something with which the Hawks are familiar. They have seen just about everything during the span that resulted in two Stanley Cups in four seasons, and that experience comes in handy in tight situations. The Predators don't have the same luxury of experienced players in big spots.

Across the rosters of both teams, 19 players have hoisted the Stanley Cup – 17 of them on the Hawks. When it comes to having been there, done that, the Hawks reign supreme over the Preds.

"We have a lot of experience," Kane said. "We've been through games whether it has been regular or postseason, a lot of us have some different experience in international play and we can take all of that into certain games. We try to stay calm, try to stay patient." ●

Kris Versteeg battles Nashville's Mattias Ekholm for the puck during the second period of Game 2, won by the Predators 6-2. (Nuccio DiNuzzo/Chicago Tribune)

Game 3
April 19, 2015
Blackhawks 4, Predators 2

REGAL 'TENDER

Darling money again, saves accolades for teammates as Hawks grab 2-1 lead

By Chris Kuc

Scott Darling has a simple way to handle this very unusual situation he has found himself in as the improbable starting goaltender – for now, at least – of the Blackhawks.

"Try and pretend like it's normal," Darling said moments after backstopping the Hawks to a 4-2 victory against the Predators in Game 3 of their first-round series at the United Center. "(And) just try to stay really excited to be here and try to do my best."

Darling's best has not only lifted the Hawks to a 2-1 advantage in the best-of-seven series, it has been record-setting. According to Elias, the rookie's shutout streak of 83 minutes, 3 seconds to begin a postseason career is a franchise mark.

The effort in Game 3, which came on the heels of a brilliant performance in Game 1 during which he made 42 saves in relief of Corey Crawford, made Darling a hit with the media as reporters surrounded him five-deep in the Hawks' dressing room after the win. It was quite a departure from his days of playing in places like Iowa, Louisiana and Florida on his path to the NHL.

"I'd be lucky if there was one person to ask me after the game," said Darling, who made 35 saves. "It's nice to talk to you guys and get it out and remind everybody that (Game 3) especially was a huge team effort. (The Predators) hardly had any Grade A scoring opportunities. The 'D' corps played unbelievable and I can't thank them enough.

"It couldn't have been a better game from the team in my first playoff start."

Coach Joel Quenneville was also pleased with the overall team effort as the Hawks rebounded after being dismantled 6-2 in Game 2 in Nashville with Crawford in goal. Jonathan Toews had a goal and an assist, Brent Seabrook, Andrew Desjardins and Brandon Saad also scored and Marian Hossa chipped in with two assists.

While Quenneville does not reveal his starting goaltender until the day before a game, it appears Darling will get another chance in Game 4.

"We'll talk about it, but certainly he did everything he could to put himself back in the net," Quenneville said. ●

Nashville's Colin Wilson gets tangled up with Blackhawks goalie Scott Darling during Game 3 of the first-round playoff series at the United Center. (Brian Cassella/Chicago Tribune)

Game 4
April 21, 2015
Blackhawks 3, Predators 2 (3OT)

GOOD MORNING

Seabrook ends marathon with winner in third overtime as
Blackhawks outlast Predators, take commanding 3-1 series lead

By Chris Kuc

Hours before taking his spot on the Blackhawks' bench, coach Joel Quenneville had an inkling that Game 4 wasn't going to be a cakewalk.

"We feel we'll have the toughest game we've faced all year (Tuesday night)," Quenneville said after the morning skate in advance of taking on the Predators at the United Center.

It certainly was one of the most intense.

Brent Seabrook scored 1 minute into triple-overtime to lift the Hawks to a marathon 3-2 victory over the Predators. With the triumph, the Hawks seized control of the best-of-seven series with a 3-1 advantage heading to Game 5 in Nashville.

Brandon Saad scored midway through the third period to pull the Hawks into a 2-2 tie with the Preds and set up the second overtime game of the series. Antoine Vermette also scored in regulation and Scott Darling was brilliant in his second career postseason start. The rookie made 50 saves to outduel Preds veteran Pekka Rinne (45 saves).

Colin Wilson and James Neal had goals for the Predators in regulation, but the Hawks' rally put Nashville on the brink of elimination.

Standing at the lectern moments after his team had suffered a heartbreaking – and series-altering – triple-overtime loss, Predators coach Peter Laviolette wanted to make one thing clear.

"Our guys are a resilient group," he said in the aftermath of the Hawks' 3-2 marathon triumph. "They will not cave and they will not go away quietly. They will be ready to play Game 5, I promise you."

The Hawks expect the Predators to deliver on that promise.

"Always the hardest game is to close out a team," veteran Hawks center Brad Richards said. "It's harder when you're up 3-1, too, because human nature is always to say you have another chance. The Predators don't. So you always talk about trying to match that desperation. But that's a lot easier said than done. The reality is if they don't win, they're out.

"You never want to give another team another chance. You know how hockey is, somebody gets life and you never know what can happen." ●

Marcus Kruger is knocked off his feet by Nashville's Victor Bartley during the Blackhawks' 3-2 triple-overtime victory in Game 4. (Nuccio DiNuzzo/Chicago Tribune)

GOALTENDER

33
SCOTT DARLING
FROM ROCK BOTTOM TO SOLID AS A ROCK

Hawks goalie Scott Darling drank himself out of
hockey before making a big save — his life

BY CHRIS HINE

After Blackhawks goaltender Scott Darling started his first NHL playoff game, he and his family gathered for dinner at a downtown steakhouse that overlooks the Chicago River.

At a nearby table sat puckish teammate Andrew Shaw, who was only too happy to out his teammate to fellow diners as the unlikely hero of the Blackhawks' 4-2 win in Game 3 of their series against the Predators.

But other than that, Darling kept the dinner low-key.

With a chance to celebrate what was the biggest athletic accomplishment of his life, he did not head to a bar or a club -- and he certainly didn't have any alcoholic drinks with his dinner.

There was a time not long ago when alcohol would have been on the menu for Darling – and a lot of it. Drinking was not only a way to party, but for Darling it was also a way to overcome his social anxiety.

But after hitting rock bottom in 2010, Darling went on to make his most important save in 2011. It was his perseverance in kicking his alcohol addiction that brought him to the Blackhawks. At the same time, it was the drive to get back into hockey that helped Darling kick a problem that nearly derailed a promising career and ruined his life.

"Fortunately for me, I was able to just make a decision (that) enough was enough," Darling said. "I just wanted better out of my life and that's what I did."

Now, he has gone from humiliation to hero for the

Blackhawks goalie Scott Darling overcame a serious drinking problem and revived his faltering hockey career in the process. (Brian Cassella/Chicago Tribune)

Hawks. It is Darling's play in net that has spurred the Hawks to a 3-1 series lead against the Predators. It's a surreal moment for Darling, who grew up a Hawks fan, and his family, who can't believe Darling finds himself at the pinnacle of hockey success after what he went through just a few years ago.

"As far as making it to the NHL I never really thought about it that far," Darling's mom, Cindy, said. "I just wanted him to be healthy, get his life together, get his life in perspective, which he did.

"And I think that because of all he's been through he just appreciates it much more."

Darling, 26, grew up in Lemont and went to Lemont High School before playing with five junior hockey clubs in Indiana, Illinois, New York and Iowa, including the Chicago Young Americans.

For Darling, the drinking began when he was in junior hockey and carried over to his early years in college. When Darling arrived at the University of Maine, he didn't seem atypical of college hockey players who liked to have fun off the ice, but Darling's drinking habits soon were seen as excessive.

"It was his sophomore year we realized for sure he had some bigger issues and needed help," said Tim Whitehead, Darling's former coach at Maine. "We tried a lot of different angles with his captains and coaches. ... We exhausted all the options."

But nothing got through to Darling.

Cindy Darling said because her son was so talented, people tended to look the other way when it came to his drinking.

And for Scott Darling, drinking was a way to compensate.

"He had a lot of not-fitting-in feelings and anxiety," Cindy said. "Lots of people choose things to make themselves feel calmer or to fit in, and that was his choice."

The problems eventually became too much and Whitehead kicked Darling off the team in 2010. Darling would then spend another year wallowing in alcohol as he washed out with the Louisiana IceGators of the Southern Professional Hockey League.

"When you bottom out like that in the Southern Professional League and they're not concerned whether you stay and you end up in the NHL, that's not an accident," Whitehead said. "He earned it every step of the way up."

Cindy remembers the day Scott told her he was making a change – July 1, 2011.

"I realized how far I had fallen in such a short period of time," Darling said. "I went from a top college prospect to jobless, no degree, didn't make anything out of my college career and no bright spots in the near future. I just had a moment of 'That's it.' I've been trying to build my way back up ever since."

Darling had to slog through lower-level professional leagues and earn his stripes. It meant losing weight, working out every day – and not drinking a drop.

He made stops in Florida and Wheeling, W.Va., in the East Coast Hockey League. He spent time with the Wilkes-Barre/Scranton Penguins and Hamilton Bulldogs of the AHL before he signed with the Predators, who gave him a chance to prove himself at their AHL affiliate in Milwaukee.

"There were definitely people that helped me along the way," Darling said. "But in a situation like that, anybody who's been through it knows it's up to the person going through it to make the decision and the decision was mine to make."

From there, he caught the eye of the Hawks, who signed him to a contract on July 1, 2014, three years to the day Darling made his commitment to turn around his life. He quickly showed his ability in Rockford before nabbing the backup gig with the Hawks, earning a two-year extension through 2017 and ultimately winning the starting job as Corey Crawford struggled in the first two games of the Predators series.

"Scott's an awesome guy," Crawford said. "He's gone through a lot to get here and he's been playing awesome. How can you not feel good for him?"

Before Thursday night's game, during the national anthem, look for Scott Darling.

He says at that moment he's thinking about all the versions of the national anthem he has heard at all the various stops he has made on his remarkable journey over the last four years.

"It reminds you of where you came from," he said. "And it reminds you to make the most of it."

The last few days have made for some anxious moments for his family, who have watched nervously from the United Center stands as Darling won Game 3 and made 50 saves in a triple-overtime victory Tuesday in Game 4. But the anxiety isn't as serious as it once was.

"He wants to be his best and he's not going to risk that," Cindy Darling said. "He's so happy, not only because of how well he's doing in hockey, but the weight of the world is off his shoulders. He's jovial. He's funny.

"He's the kid I always knew was in there."

A kid who has grown up. ●

"I realized how far I had fallen in such a short period of time," said Hawks goalie Scott Darling, recalling his 2011 decision to quit drinking. "I just had a moment of 'That's it.'" (Chris Sweda/Chicago Tribune)

WESTERN CONFERENCE QUARTERFINALS

Game 5
April 23, 2015
Predators 5, Blackhawks 2

STRIKE ONE

With 3 shots to finish off Preds,
Hawks swing, miss

By Chris Kuc

With two "if necessary" games at their disposal, the Blackhawks could afford to leave Nashville without a victory. They just had no desire to do so.

"You don't want to play an extra shift, you don't want to play an extra game in the playoffs if you can avoid it," coach Joel Quenneville said before they took the ice against the Predators in Game 5 at Bridgestone Arena.

The Hawks couldn't avoid it.

Filip Forsberg scored three times, James Neal had a goal and an assist and Colin Wilson also scored while Pekka Rinne was stellar in goal to lead the Predators to a 5-2 victory before a crowd of 17,238. With a three-goal explosion early in the third period, the Predators staved off elimination and trimmed the Hawks' advantage in the best-of-seven series to 3-2 with Game 6 at the United Center.

"I think if you told us we'd be up 3-2 heading back to our building for Game 6, we'd be excited about that and we'd take that at the beginning of the series," Hawks winger Patrick Kane said afterward. "We still feel we're in a good situation."

Brad Richards and Kris Versteeg scored for the Hawks, but it wasn't nearly enough as goalie Scott Darling was shelled in his third career postseason start. The rookie yielded four goals on 28 Predators shots, including three scores on the first five shots he faced to open the third.

"They came out pretty hard with quick goals," Darling said. "I have to make a couple of saves there."

"I'm not blaming the goalie," Hawks coach Joel Quenneville said. "(Darling) did everything right. He was fine."

Facing the end to their season, the Preds grew more desperate as the game went along, and once they snapped a 1-1 tie on Neal's goal 47 seconds into the third, they began to roll. The onslaught, including Forsberg's first career postseason hat trick, allowed them to live to fight another day.

"There was pressure to close it out," Richards said. "(You) feel pressure any time you're trying to close it out. You know that every game that keeps going, there's a better chance that it goes seven." ●

Patrick Kane reacts after a penalty was called on teammate Brent Seabrook during the Hawks' 5-2 loss to the Predators in Game 5 of the first-round playoff series. (Chris Sweda/Chicago Tribune)

WESTERN CONFERENCE QUARTERFINALS

Game 6
April 25, 2015
Blackhawks 4, Predators 3

PHEW! WHAT A RELIEF

Crawford takes over for Darling;
Keith nets winner

By Chris Kuc

The Blackhawks' brightest stars made sure there was no Game 7 in Nashville.

Patrick Kane, Jonathan Toews, Patrick Sharp, Duncan Keith and Corey Crawford – yes, Crawford – led the charge as the Hawks rallied to a thrilling 4-3 victory over the Predators in Game 6 at the United Center. The Hawks clinched the best-of-seven first-round series 4-2 and now await the winner of the Blues-Wild series to determine their next opponent.

Keith scored the game-winner late in the third period and also added two assists, Toews had a goal and two assists while Sharp and Kane each added a goal and an assist to turn a 2-0 first-period deficit into the win in front of a frenzied crowd of 22,171.

"Our top guys were special," coach Joel Quenneville said. "Certainly our guys, when the games are on the line (and) the stakes are higher, they just love that challenge and like to meet it and rise to it."

Crawford, who had yielded the starting goaltending job to Scott Darling after a rough first two games of the series, came on in relief of the rookie midway through the opening period and stopped all 13 shots sent his way.

"You have to always be ready; anything can happen," Crawford said. "I was just trying to get a feel for it, trying to get back in the zone. The first (shot) clipped off my glove and hit the post and it almost shocked me a little bit."

After a frenetic first period that ended with the game tied at 3-3, the teams buckled down defensively before Keith wired in a shot from the left point with 3 minutes, 48 seconds remaining.

"They scored off a couple of quick plays that I don't think they had to work too hard for," Keith said. "We knew there was lots of time and we've got confidence in our offensive ability as a team. We showed that."

The Hawks also showed that if they play well in front of their goalie, it doesn't much matter who is manning the crease. Darling was bombarded with 12 shots in 9:59 of play, but once Quenneville replaced him with Crawford, the Hawks came alive.

"It wasn't a position we wanted to be in but we did a great job of getting ourselves back in the game," Kane said. "It was a huge comeback." ●

Nashville defenseman Seth Jones takes down Brandon Saad during the Blackhawks' decisive 4-3 victory in Game 6 of the first-round playoff series. (Nuccio DiNuzzo/Chicago Tribune)

Corey Crawford drops down
to make a save during the
series-clinching Game 6 against
Nashville at the United Center.
Crawford entered the game in
the second period in relief of
Scott Darling. (Nuccio DiNuzzo/
Chicago Tribune)

SECOND ROUND 4-0 OVER THE WILD

In what's becoming an annual ritual, the Hawks ran into the Wild, who were determined after the Hawks ended their season the last two seasons. It didn't quite work out for the Wild. The Hawks took care of business in the first two games at the United Center. Crawford pitched a shutout in Game 3 at the Xcel Energy Center as the Hawks rode a Patrick Kane power-play goal to a 1-0 victory. With the Wild on the ropes, the Hawks didn't let them come back, finishing off the series in Game 4 after withstanding a late Wild charge. The Hawks earned nine days off by finishing the series so quickly.

GAME 1: HAWKS: 4, WILD 3
GAME 2: HAWKS: 4, WILD 1
GAME 3: HAWKS 1, WILD 0
GAME 4: HAWKS 4, WILD 3

Brandon Saad gets ready to celebrate with his teammates after scoring a goal in the Blackhawks' 4-3 win over Minnesota in Game 1 of the second-round playoff series. (Anthony Souffle/ Chicago Tribune)

Game 1
May 1, 2015
Blackhawks 4, Wild 3

STARTING GAIT

Hawks come out running, pepper
Dubnyk to open series with win

By Chris Kuc

Devan Dubnyk looms as the biggest obstacle the Blackhawks must overcome if they want to advance past the Wild.

The goaltender was arguably the NHL's most valuable player in the second half of the season and had a head of steam entering Game 1 of the Western Conference semifinals at the United Center.

It took the Hawks all of one shot to solve Dubnyk, five to do it again and seven to take a three-goal lead in the series opener.

In the end, it was a shaky Dubnyk who allowed the Hawks to escape with a 4-3 victory in front of 21,851 to draw first blood in the best-of-seven series.

After blowing a 3-0 lead entering the second period, the Hawks pulled it out behind goals from Brandon Saad, Patrick Kane, Marcus Kruger and Teuvo Teravainen. Corey Crawford benefited from all that offense to pick up the win in his first start since April 17.

Zach Parise had a goal and an assist, and Jason Zucker and Mikael Granlund also scored for the Wild. But Dubnyk, a finalist for the Vezina Trophy, was off his game.

Only eight teams still harbor hopes of hoisting the Stanley Cup, a fact that is not lost on the Hawks.

"All 30 teams at the start of the year have the goal to win the Stanley Cup," winger Patrick Sharp said. "As the season goes along, half of the teams actually believe they can do it. We're definitely a team that feels that we can go all the way. It's a privilege to still be playing."

While they were good during their first-round series against the Predators, the Hawks know they need to get better.

"You have to be at your best to move along here in the playoffs," coach Joel Quenneville said. "You're beating teams that are playing well, and the reason they're playing deeper in the playoffs is the success that they're having. Our game in the first round got better as we went along, and we have to improve off of those levels.

"We know how tough Minnesota is and what they've accomplished and the excitement they've achieved by making the playoffs and winning a round." ●

Minnesota's Zach Parise battles Niklas Hjalmarsson along the boards during the Blackhawks' 4-3 victory in Game 1 of the second-round series at the United Center. (Anthony Souffle/Chicago Tribune)

WESTERN CONFERENCE SEMIFINALS

Game 2
May 3, 2015
Blackhawks 4, Wild 1

THEIR BEST SHOT

Led by Kane's 2 goals, Hawks' top players
give it their all to take 2-0 series lead

By Chris Kuc

As the old hockey adage goes, a team's best players need to be its best players come playoff time.

The Blackhawks' best have been better than the Wild so far in their second-round series, and that was especially true in Game 2 at the United Center when Patrick Kane had two goals, Patrick Sharp added a goal and an assist and Jonathan Toews also scored to propel the Hawks to a 4-1 victory in front of 21,934 delighted fans.

"Consistently, game in and game out it's been our best players leading the charge," coach Joel Quenneville said. "Playing the right way and making their linemates better (is) how you have success as a team."

Throw in big efforts from Corey Crawford, Duncan Keith and Marian Hossa, among others, and the Hawks surged to a 2-0 advantage in the best-of-seven series that will continue Tuesday night in Minnesota.

As usual, Kane led the way as the winger's two goals gave him 101 points in 101 career postseason games.

"You hear so much about playoff hockey when you come into the league: 'It's more intense, it's the best hockey to play, every game is do-or-die,'" Kane said. "I've been fortunate enough to play with some great teammates where you're getting a lot of good chances. I've had a lot of fun here in my seven years in the playoffs.

"Right now we're not really worried about numbers," Kane added. "We're worried about taking care of business, getting the wins. We did that twice here at home. We got the job done here."

The Hawks were able to solve Wild goaltender Devan Dubnyk three times – Kane's second score was into an empty net – while Crawford was solid at the other end by making 30 stops.

Sparked by Toews' short-handed goal off after a terrific steal and pass from Hossa midway through the second, the Hawks took command and improved to 5-0 at the UC during the postseason.

"You have to have guys who want to elevate their game this time of year and be the guy to score that big goal," Sharp said. "We have that in our locker room." ●

Patrick Sharp (left) celebrates with teammates after scoring a third-period goal in the Blackhawks' 4-1 victory over Minnesota in Game 2 of the second-round playoff series. (Nuccio DiNuzzo/Chicago Tribune)

WESTERN CONFERENCE SEMIFINALS

Game 3
May 5, 2015
Blackhawks 1, Wild 0

CROW'S FEAT

Crawford stands tall, makes Kane's
goal hold up for 3-0 series lead

By Chris Kuc

Corey Crawford not only ended the Blackhawks' Game 3 curse, the goaltender put the State of Hockey in a state of despair in the process.

Crawford made 30 saves, many of them brilliant, and Patrick Kane scored a power-play goal in the first period to lift the Hawks to a 1-0 victory over the Wild in Game 3 of their second-round playoff series at the Xcel Energy Center.

The Hawks snapped a seven-game losing streak in Game 3s on the road and improved to 2-9 in such situations under coach Joel Quenneville.

It wasn't easy.

From the opening puck drop, the Wild played with the desperation of a team that had lost the first two games, but Crawford turned aside everything sent his way to outduel Devan Dubnyk.

"We kept them out of the slot for the most part, especially the third period," said Crawford, who recorded his fourth career playoff shutout. "Where it could have been dangerous plays, we got pucks out."

Helping Crawford was a tenacious penalty kill that shut down the Wild's power play three times. It was part of an overall strong defensive effort by the Hawks, who hold a 3-0 lead in a series for the first time since they swept the Sharks in the 2010 Western Conference final.

In the end, it was Crawford who was the difference in Game 3 as he continued his stellar play in the series, having now stopped 90 of 94 shots.

"Crawford, he's a star against us," Wild coach Mike Yeo said. "He's (Martin) Brodeur; he's (Patrick) Roy. He's everybody against (us), so we have to find a way to solve that."

History is on the Hawks' side: Only four teams in NHL history have come back from a 3-0 deficit to win a playoff series. They are 10-0 all time when leading a best-of-seven series 3-0.

"It's nice, but we can't get complacent or let up," Crawford said. "That team is going to play even harder next game. We have to do the same thing." ●

Corey Crawford stops Zach Parise from point-blank range, one of 30 saves Crawford made in a 1-0 shutout of the Wild in Game 3 of the second-round playoff series in St. Paul. (Brian Cassella/Chicago Tribune)

Game 4

May 7, 2015

Blackhawks 4, Wild 3

BROOM SERVICE

Finishing off sweep of Wild is exactly what Hawks ordered

By Chris Kuc

Goodbye Predators and Wild, hello Western Conference final.

The Blackhawks brought out the brooms and swept away the Wild with a thrilling 4-3 victory in Game 4 of their second-round series at Xcel Energy Center. Patrick Kane had a goal and an assist, Brent Seabrook, Andrew Shaw and Marian Hossa also scored and Corey Crawford continued his stellar play in goal as the Hawks blew past the Wild in the best-of-seven set and now await the winner of the Ducks-Flames series.

Crawford withstood a furious Wild rally in the waning minutes to earn the victory and help the Hawks improve to 13-0 all time in series during which they captured the first three games. The Hawks reached the conference finals for the third consecutive season and fifth time in the last seven.

The victory came at a steep price as veteran defenseman Michal Rozsival suffered a potentially serious ankle injury in the second period. After stumbling and having his ankle buckle underneath him, Rozsival was helped off the ice. After the game, coach Joel Quenneville said, "It doesn't look good."

While that put a damper on the celebration, the Hawks still were excited about moving one step away from playing for the Stanley Cup.

"Our goal is to win the Cup, so we battled hard to get to this point and we have to continue playing the way we do or get even better," Crawford said.

The Hawks' success in recent seasons can be attributed to a core group that includes Kane, Keith, Seabrook, Hossa, Patrick Sharp and Jonathan Toews. Those players were the Hawks' best throughout the first-round series against the Predators and then the Wild.

"We're very fortunate to have those guys," general manager Stan Bowman said. "Most teams would love to have one or two of them and we have several of them who are just elite players who are able to play their best hockey in the biggest moments.

"We were close last year and we didn't quite get it done. That's driving everyone."

Said Kane: "You're in one of those positions where you realize who knows how many opportunities you'll have like this in the playoffs when you have a good team with you. (We're) enjoying the process, enjoying the game and then taking what's next on the list after that." ●

Minnesota's Matt Dumba flattens Blackhawks forward Patrick Kane during Game 4 of the second-round playoff series. The Hawks went on to win 4-3 and sweep the series. (Brian Cassella/Chicago Tribune)

Goalie Corey Crawford (second from left) is congratulated by teammates after the Blackhawks' Game 4 victory in St. Paul. The Hawks swept the second-round series against Minnesota to advance to the Western Conference final. (Brian Cassella/Chicago Tribune)

WEST FINALS
4-3 OVER THE DUCKS

The physical Ducks made a big deal about wearing down the Hawks should it last six or seven games. They got to test their theory after taking a 3-2 series lead in an overtime thriller in Game 5. But the Hawks dominated the next 120 minutes. In Game 6, the Hawks scored three consecutive goals in the second period en route to victory. With the series returning to Anaheim, the Ducks faced the prospect of losing a Game 7 at home for the third consecutive season – which they did. Two first-period goals by Jonathan Toews paved the way for the Hawks to reach the Stanley Cup Final.

GAME 1: DUCKS 4, HAWKS 1
GAME 2: HAWKS 3, DUCKS 2 (3OT)
GAME 3: DUCKS 2, HAWKS 1
GAME 4: HAWKS 5, DUCKS 4 (2OT)
GAME 5: DUCKS 5, HAWKS 4 (OT)
GAME 6: HAWKS 5, DUCKS 2
GAME 7: HAWKS 5, DUCKS 3

Despite being in enemy territory, Blackhawks fans boldly show their colors - and their spirit - during Game 1 of the Western Conference final in Anaheim. (Brian Cassella/Chicago Tribune)

Game 1
May 17, 2015
Ducks 4, Blackhawks 1

FIRST ALERT

No cause for alarm: Hawks confident despite setback

The puck on his stick and the goal wide open, Patrick Kane was set to give the Blackhawks a critical early lead over the Ducks in Game 1 of the Western Conference finals.

At the last instant, Ducks goaltender Frederik Andersen came out of nowhere, diving to get his stick on the first-period shot, sending it out of harm's way. A short time later, the Ducks scored and the Hawks were trailing a game they had dominated to that point.

After never trailing in a game at any point in the second round against the Wild, it was unfamiliar territory for the Hawks. They were in a worse position a couple of hours later as they fell behind in a series for the first time this postseason, with the Ducks winning 4-1 at the Honda Center.

"I thought I did everything right on the play," Kane said. "(Andersen) just had his stick there. It would have been nice to get that chance and bury it to give us the lead. We had a good start to the game. We did everything we wanted to come out and play that way."

It wasn't enough and it became evident early on that the Ducks are not the Predators or the Wild.

"We expected (the Ducks) to be a good team," Kane said. "I don't think by any means did we come in and expect to steal and take wins from them. It's going to be a fight for us. We have to realize that and realize this is the best team we've faced yet."

"We can't panic out there, it's a long series – it's seven games," said Hawks winger Brandon Saad. "We've just got to take the positives and move on. Tomorrow's another day. Stay positive."

The Ducks were feeling pretty positive after the game, but they know it's far from over.

"It's one game and we've got three more to go," center Ryan Kesler said. "We thought we could beat this team before the series, so this game wasn't a, 'yeah, we can beat these guys!' Game 2 is huge. I'm sure they're over there saying they want a split and to get back home. It's our job not to allow that." ●

It takes a swarm of Ducks to hold back Blackhawks forward Andrew Shaw as he hovers over goalie Frederik Andersen during Anaheim's 4-1 victory in Game 1 of the Western Conference final. (Brian Cassella/Chicago Tribune)

WESTERN CONFERENCE FINALS

Game 2
May 19, 2015
Blackhawks 3, Ducks 2 (3OT)

NIGHT CAPPER

Kruger's winning goal ends longest contest in Blackhawks history

Game 2 of the Western Conference finals between the Blackhawks and Ducks came to a head – literally – late in the second overtime at the Honda Center.

After an apparent goal was disallowed because Andrew Shaw had headbutted the puck into the net – a no-no according to NHL rule No. 78.5 – Marcus Kruger scored for real 16 minutes, 12 seconds into the third overtime to give the Hawks a 3-2 victory. It ended a marathon contest that was the longest in Hawks franchise history and sent 40 exhausted players and 17,234 fans to the exits.

Kruger's goal past Ducks goalie Frederik Andersen allowed the Hawks to even the best-of-seven series at 1-1 with Game 3 at the United Center. The Hawks seized home-ice advantage in the series by thwarting a Ducks comeback. Shaw and Marian Hossa scored for the Hawks in regulation and Corey Crawford was sensational in goal to record the victory.

After trailing 2-0 early, the relentless Ducks got goals from Andrew Cogliano and Corey Perry to pull into a tie, but Crawford shut them down the rest of the way as the Ducks lost for the first time at home in the playoffs.

The discussion among both teams in the aftermath of Game 1 was that each could raise the level of their games.

They both did in the heart-thumping Game 2.

"Every game is important," Hawks winger Patrick Sharp said before the game. "When you look at the series, how it's playing out, 1-0, 2-0, 3-0, it doesn't matter, you try to win every night you go on the ice and play with that urgency, play with that desperation."

With both teams showing that urgency, the result was a fast-paced, bruising affair that left little doubt the final outcome would be decided late – 1:08 a.m. Chicago time, to be exact.

Those 116 minutes of hockey had to feel even longer for the Ducks, who let this happen at home. They would have a four-hour flight to ponder a nagging question: How do we recover from this? ●

Ducks defenseman smacks Andrew Shaw during Game 2 of the Western Conference final. No penalty was called. The Blackhawks evened the series with a 3-2 victory in triple overtime. (Brian Cassella/Chicago Tribune)

After winning the longest game in franchise history, the Blackhawks still have enough energy to celebrate – barely. Andrew Shaw (second from right) puts an arm around Marcus Kruger, who scored in triple overtime to give the Hawks a 3-2 victory. (Brian Cassella/Chicago Tribune)

Game 3
May 21, 2015
Ducks 2, Blackhawks 1

WAKE-UP CALL

Hawks follow late-night win with sleepy home loss, trail 2-1 in series

If the Blackhawks and Ducks have proved anything during the Western Conference finals, it's that at this stage of the postseason, home-ice advantage isn't much of a help at all.

After seizing home ice with their marathon victory in Game 2 in Anaheim – the Ducks' first loss at home in the playoffs – the Hawks coughed it right back up when they took a 2-1 loss in Game 3 at the United Center.

It marked the first time the Hawks had lost at home in the postseason and gave the Ducks a 2-1 advantage in the best-of-seven series.

"You have to win four games; it doesn't really matter where you win them," Hawks defenseman Brent Seabrook said. "We have to be the first to four. We have to come out and have a big effort in Game 4 and try to even this thing up."

Patrick Maroon and Simon Despres scored and goaltender Frederik Andersen made the scores stand up with 28 saves. Patrick Kane broke through with his first goal of the series – and it was a typical highlight-reel effort - but that was all the offense Hawks could manage.

Special teams played a big role – especially in the opening period – with the Ducks cashing in on their only power play in the first 20 minutes.

With Marian Hossa off for holding, Hampus Lindholm's shot from the point sailed through traffic until it reached Maroon, who redirected it through Crawford's pads to give the Ducks a 1-0 lead at the 12 minute, 55 second mark.

Meanwhile, the Hawks misfired with six minutes of man advantages, including four consecutive when Jakob Silfverberg was whistled for a high stick that drew blood from Hawks captain Jonathan Toews. They had a total of two shots on goal with a man advantage in the period.

Playing at home for the first time in 18 days, the Hawks came away empty on five power plays after scoring two power-play goals during their 3-2 triple-overtime victory in Game 2.

"Their power play capitalized and ours didn't," Seabrook said. "We have to be better out of the starting gate." ●

Ducks defenseman Francois Beauchemin shoves Blackhawks center Jonathan Toews into goalie Frederik Andersen during Anaheim's 2-1 win in Game 3 of the Western Conference final at the United Center. (Nuccio DiNuzzo/Chicago Tribune)

Joakim Nordstrom tries to step over a prone Corey Perry during Game 3 of the Western Conference final at the United Center. Anaheim won 2-1 to take the lead in the series. (Nuccio DiNuzzo/Chicago Tribune)

Game 4
May 23, 2015
Blackhawks 5, Ducks 4 (2OT)

80'S NIGHT

Vermette scores winner to end another marathon as Hawks even up series

Sitting in the dressing room just moments after another momentous Blackhawks victory, Patrick Kane said it best: "In the playoffs, anything can happen."

In Game 4 of the Western Conference finals at a jacked-up United Center, pretty much everything happened.

Antoine Vermette, who was a healthy scratch in Game 3, scored 5 minutes, 37 seconds into double overtime to propel the Hawks to a 5-4 victory over the Ducks in front of a season-high 22,404 fans who left the arena sans fingernails. The Hawks evened an already epic best-of-seven series at 2-2 heading into Game 5 in Anaheim.

That Game 4 reached double overtime was a story in itself. The Hawks have been involved in some wild third periods in recent postseasons – remember those 17 seconds against the Bruins in 2013? – but what happened Saturday had those in the building shaking their heads – and the building itself shaking.

With the score tied at 1-1 after two, the Hawks jumped ahead on goals by Jonathan Toews and Brent Seabrook and appeared headed to what would have been your average, everyday thrill-ride victory.

Then the Ducks happened. Anaheim reeled off three goals in 37 seconds – from Ryan Kesler, Matt Beleskey and Corey Perry – to shock the Hawks and the crowd.

That set up a need for more heroics, and the usual suspect, Kane, came to the Hawks' rescue with a power-play goal with 7:21 remaining to tie it.

"It was crazy," Kane said. "We felt like we were in a great position at 3-1 and they scored a few quick ones and we were back on our heels a little bit."

Make that a lot, but Kane scored his ninth goal of the playoffs to send the game to a doubly extended overtime affair after Game 2 went to three extra sessions.

"We worked hard to get to where we were in the third period with a 3-1 lead," said Toews, who had a goal and an assist. "When it rains it pours, in some moments especially (Saturday night) for us in the third. I think a lot of teams wouldn't feel too good about themselves. We had the character and the poise to relax and calm ourselves down, make a game of it, find a way to get back into it." ●

Corey Crawford tries to corral the puck during the first overtime of Game 4 of the Western Conference final at the United Center. Antoine Vermette scored in the second overtime to give the Hawks a series-tying 5-4 victory. (Nuccio DiNuzzo/Chicago Tribune)

Blackhawks defenseman Johnny Oduya battles with
Anaheim's Corey Perry during Game 4 of the Western
Conference final. Perry was one of three Ducks who scored
in a span of 37 seconds during the third period to erase a
3-1 Hawks lead. The Hawks won 5-4 in double overtime.
(Chris Sweda/Chicago Tribune)

Game 5
May 25, 2015
Ducks 5, Blackhawks 4 (OT)

AW, DUCKS

Toews keeps hope alive with two late goals, but Ducks win in OT, push Hawks to brink

The Blackhawks simply ran out of miracles. After staging a pair of dramatic comebacks – including one in the final two minutes of regulation – the Hawks find themselves on the brink of elimination after falling to the Ducks 5-4 in overtime in Game 5 of the Western Conference final at the Honda Center.

Matt Beleskey scored 45 seconds into overtime to lift the Ducks to victory after they had squandered leads of 3-0 and 4-2. Anaheim can close out the series in Game 6 at the United Center.

That is easier said than done as the Ducks keep learning the hard way that there is no quit in the Hawks. Trailing by three goals just 14:37 into the opening period, the Hawks kept coming and eventually pulled into a tie when Jonathan Toews scored twice in the waning moments of regulation to force the third overtime game of the series.

"You never want to go down three goals right off the bat, but I think we always show that we can find ways to dig ourselves out of those holes," Toews said. "Going into overtime, we feel the game is in our hands, we're going to get that next break. It's unfortunate that we couldn't take advantage of it."

Beleskey ended it when he banged a rebound of a Ryan Kesler shot past Hawks goaltender Corey Crawford.

"That's the biggest goal I've ever scored," Beleskey said. "It's a great feeling, especially here at home. We're one game away from a Stanley Cup berth."

Cam Fowler, Kesler, Sami Vatanen and Patrick Maroon scored in regulation and a shaky Frederik Andersen did just enough in goal.

Teuvo Teravainen and Brent Seabrook each had a goal and an assist, but it marked the first time in 15 games during Joel Quenneville's tenure as coach that the Hawks lost a Game 5 or 6 after a series was tied at 2-2.

Toews pulled the Hawks to within a goal with 1:50 remaining in the third period when he scored off a one-timer from the left circle following a pass from Marian Hossa. The captain struck again with 37.2 seconds left when he sent a shot across the goal line that deflected off Andersen and in.

The Hawks know they will need to play better in Game 6 or their season will be over.

"We feel that we're a tough team to get rid of," Toews said. ●

Brandon Saad winds up on his back after rushing the net during Game 5 of the Western Conference final in Anaheim. The Ducks won 5-4 in overtime. (Chris Sweda/Chicago Tribune)

Patrick Kane and the Blackhawks fought back with two late goals to tie Game 5, but Matt Beleskey scored in overtime to give Anaheim a 5-4 victory and a 3-2 lead in the Western Conference final. (Chris Sweda/Chicago Tribune)

Game 6
May 27, 2015
Blackhawks 5, Ducks 2

GOING THE DISTANCE

It's back to California as Hawks come alive,
force a deciding Game 7

If ever a series deserved to go to a Game 7, it is this one.

After each game of what has turned out to be an epic Western Conference finals, players on the Blackhawks and Ducks have stressed they were in it for the long haul.

The Hawks made that a reality with a convincing 5-2 victory in Game 6 at the United Center. The triumph set up a showdown between heavyweights who have exchanged haymakers since Game 1. With the series tied 3-3, the teams will decide who will advance to the Stanley Cup Final when they take the ice for Game 7 in Anaheim.

"You knew it wasn't going to take four or five, you knew it was going to be a grind to the end," Hawks winger Bryan Bickell said after the Hawks reached Game 7 in the conference finals for the second consecutive year..

Before the game, captain Jonathan Toews said he didn't plan on any rah-rah speeches in preparation for what might have been the Hawks' final contest of the season.

"Anything over the top just adds to any sort of anxiety," Toews said. "We know to expect every guy in here to be ready and to bring their best game."

Led by Duncan Keith, they did.

The veteran defenseman didn't score a goal, but he did just about everything else. Keith had three assists and a plus-3 rating in a game-high 28 minutes, 35 seconds of ice time. Oh, and the two-time Norris Trophy winner made perhaps the biggest save of the game when he scooped up a loose puck headed toward the goal line with the Hawks clinging to a 3-2 lead in the third period.

"There are nights when you look at the scoresheet and you see how great he can be, how pivotal, how much he means to our team, especially in these big games," Toews said of his teammate.

Keith didn't do it single-handedly as Andrew Shaw had two goals, Patrick Kane had a goal and an assist and Marian Hossa added a score as did Brandon Saad. Corey Crawford was strong in goal with 30 saves.

"That was obviously our biggest game of the year," said Crawford, still breathing hard while standing in front of his dressing room stall after making 12 stops in the third period as the Ducks kept coming. "We have to keep rolling here." ●

The Blackhawks celebrate what turned out to be the decisive goal in their 5-2 victory over Anaheim in Game 6 of the Western Conference final at the United Center. (Anthony Souffle/Chicago Tribune)

Andrew Shaw celebrates one of the two goals he
scored during the Blackhawks' do-or-die victory in
Game 6 of the Western Conference final. (Anthony
Souffle/Chicago Tribune)

Game 7
May 30, 2015
Blackhawks 5, Ducks 3

BACK 4 MORE

Blackhawks returning to Stanley Cup Final for 3rd time in 6 seasons as Toews, Hawks start fast, never slow down in series-clinching win

By Chris Kuc

Next stop: Stanley Cup Final.

The Blackhawks cleared the last – and most treacherous by far – hurdle and are headed to their third finals in six seasons after trouncing the Ducks 5-3 in Game 7 of the Western Conference final at the Honda Center.

Jonathan Toews, who earlier in the week called playing in a Game 7 "the ultimate challenge to see what you've got as a player," accepted that challenge and continued to show the hockey world exactly what he has as the captain led the way with two goals.

The Hawks will face the Eastern Conference champion Tampa Bay Lightning in the Cup final with Game 1 at Amalie Arena in Tampa.

In a rather anticlimactic finale to one of the most hard-fought and entertaining series in recent memory, the Hawks dominated a Ducks team that for the third straight season was eliminated in a Game 7 at home.

In addition to Toews' two goals to open the scoring and put the Ducks on their heels from midway through the first period to the postgame handshake line, Brandon Saad, Marian Hossa and Brent Seabrook also scored. Patrick Kane had three assists, Brad Richards and Duncan Keith each added two helpers while Corey Crawford stood tall in goal to help the Hawks exorcise the demons of their stunning Game 7 overtime loss to the Kings in the conference finals a year ago.

The Ducks came out flying in the opening minutes and tested Crawford early. Despite the buzzing, the goalie held strong and it was the Hawks who struck first.

Toews silenced the home crowd when he opened the scoring after Kane skated the puck deep into the Ducks zone, slammed on the brakes and fed Niklas Hjalmarsson with a pass. Ducks goaltender Frederik Andersen denied the defenseman's attempt but Toews pounced and cleaned up the rebound by shoveling it into the net.

Toews came through again to extend the Hawks' lead to 2-0. While on the power play, Toews took a pass from Richards and with Andrew Shaw engaged

Jonathan Toews exults after scoring one of his two-first period goals during Game 7 of the Western Conference final. The Blackhawks went on to win 5-3, earning a berth in the Stanley Cup final. (Anthony Souffle/Chicago Tribune)

in a battle with Francois Beauchemin in front, Toews rifled a wrist shot from the top of the right circle past the screened Andersen.

Early in the second, the Hawks struck again to race to a three-goal edge. Johnny Oduya made a strong play to keep the puck in the offensive zone and it bounced to Kane, who advanced it to a wide-open Saad for the winger to flip it into the gaping net.

The rout was on in the second when Hossa made it 4-0. Richards took the puck hard to the net, and after Andersen made the initial stop, the goalie slid the puck toward Hossa where it went off the veteran winger's skate and across the goal line.

Late in the period, the Ducks got one back on a Ryan Kesler goal. Then Corey Perry scored at the 11:36 mark of the third, but Seabrook put it away about two minutes later with a blast from the point on the power play to make it 5-2. Matt Beleskey ended the scoring in the final minute with a power-play goal.

Game 7 capped an amazing series.

"You know what? I asked the question (Thursday) to somebody, I said, 'Has this been a good series?'" Ducks coach Bruce Boudreau said. "They laughed at me. They said, 'Are you kidding? It has been as good as it gets.' You don't notice it (because) you're playing game to game."

Hawks coach Joel Quenneville agreed that the series was special.

"When you review the games, watch them, all of a sudden it takes on an element of this is pretty entertaining stuff," he said. "It's an amazing series. The consistency, the battle, predictability, the dangerousness ... the pace, it has been great." ●

The Western Conference champion Blackhawks pose around the Clarence S. Campbell Trophy — but choose not to touch it, adhering to superstition —after their Game 7 victory over the Ducks in Anaheim. (Anthony Souffle/ Chicago Tribune)

CHICAGO SPORTS

STARTING GAIT

Hawks come out running, pepper Dubnyk to open series with win

CHICAGO SPORTS

Their best shot

Kane scores pair, top players lead the charge as Hawks go up 2-0 in series

Hoping for right mindset

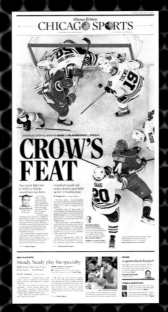

CHICAGO SPORTS

CROW'S FEAT

Crawford stands tall, Hawks' lead built up to 3-0 series lead

Steady, heady play his specialty

CHICAGO SPORTS

BROOM SERVICE

Blackhawks complete the sweep, advance to conference finals

Illinois saves its best for last

Boylan 'proud' of Bulls stint

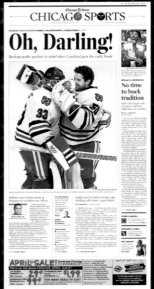

CHICAGO SPORTS

Oh, Darling!

Backup goalie perfect in relief after Crawford gets the early hook

No time to buck tradition

Rickety split for Hawks

In shaky 3rd, Predators turn up heat to even series

Driving forward despite detours

It'll be better

Bryant gives Cubs fans reasons to cheer despite a shaky start

Some guarded optimism

CHICAGO SPORTS

REGAL 'TENDER

Darling money again, saves accolades for teammates as Hawks grab 2-1 lead

Rookie looks like state of the art in goal for Hawks

CHICAGO SPORTS

Good morning

Seabrook ends marathon with winner in third overtime

Taking one for the double team

CHICAGO SPORTS

Rose gives sneak preview

STRIKE ONE

May be Crawford's turn after Darling, or takes

With 3 shots to finish off Preds, Hawks swing, miss

Sox caught in Royal rumble

CHICAGO SPORTS

People

Four gone conclusion

Buzzer-beating loss 'all on' Rose

Pair of Sox suspended

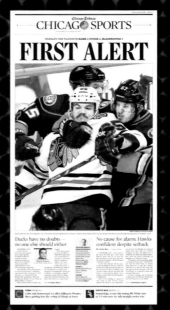

CHICAGO SPORTS

FIRST ALERT

Ducks have no doubts no one else should either

No cause for alarm: Hawks confident despite setback

CHICAGO SPORTS

NIGHT CAPPER

MEMORIAL DAY WEEKEND!

Men in the middle

Chicago Tribune CHICAGO SPORTS

WESTERN CONFERENCE FINALS GAME 3: DUCKS 2, BLACKHAWKS 1

WAKE-UP CALL

Hawks follow late-night win with sleepy home loss, trail 2-1 in series

By Chris Kuc | Chicago Tribune

Blackhawks captain Jonathan Toews heads off the ice after Thursday night's Game 3 loss to the Ducks at the United Center.

Coach Q's move leaves Hawks asleep at switch

DAVID HAUGH
In the Wake of the News

Chicago Tribune CHICAGO SPORTS

WESTERN CONFERENCE FINALS GAME 4: BLACKHAWKS 5, DUCKS 4 (3OT)

80'S NIGHT

Vermette scores winner to end another marathon as Hawks even out series

By Chris Kuc | Chicago Tribune

Season (or dynasty?) nearly vanish in seconds before Vermette saves day

DAVID HAUGH
In the Wake of the News

Pace gambles and loses

Unnecessary risk on McDonald backfires badly on Bears

BRAD BIGGS

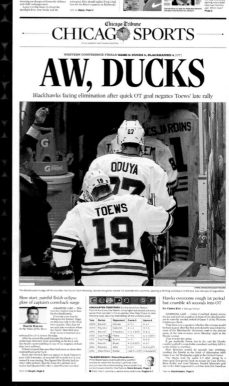

Chicago Tribune CHICAGO SPORTS

WESTERN CONFERENCE FINALS GAME 5: DUCKS 5, BLACKHAWKS 4 (OT)

AW, DUCKS

Blackhawks facing elimination after quick OT goal negates Toews' late rally

The Blackhawks trudge off the ice after the Ducks' Matt Beleskey started the game-winner in seconds into overtime, spoiling a thrilling comeback in the last two minutes of regulation.

Slow start, painful finish eclipse glow of captain's comeback surge

DAVID HAUGH
In the Wake of the News

By Chris Kuc | Chicago Tribune

Hawks overcome rough 1st period but crumble 45 seconds into OT

By Chris Kuc | Chicago Tribune

Chicago Tribune CHICAGO SPORTS

WESTERN CONFERENCE FINALS GAME 6: BLACKHAWKS 5, DUCKS 3

Going distance

It's back to California as Hawks come alive, force a deciding Game 7

By E.C. Johnson | Chicago Tribune

Andrew Shaw celebrates after the first of his two goals in the third period of the Blackhawks' 5-3 victory over the Ducks.

By taking the fight to Ducks, Hawks get shot at redemption

DAVID HAUGH
In the Wake of the News

Thibs' tenure teetering

Good chance he'll be finished as coach by Friday

BY K.C. JOHNSON

Chicago Tribune CHICAGO SPORTS

WESTERN CONFERENCE FINALS GAME 7: BLACKHAWKS 5, DUCKS 3

BACK 4 MORE

Blackhawks returning to Stanley Cup Final for 3rd time in 6 seasons

Hawks captain Jonathan Toews celebrates after scoring the first goal Saturday.

A serial thriller: Captain Clutch shows how to get the job done

DAVID HAUGH
In the Wake of the News

Toews, Hawks start fast, never slow down in series-clinching win

By Chris Kuc | Chicago Tribune